Songs from Spirit

Edited by
Larry G. Wayne
and
Grace P. Johnston

Detselig Enterprises Ltd.
Calgary, Alberta

© 1990 **Larry G. Wayne** and
Grace P. Johnston

Canadian Cataloguing in Publication Data

Main entry under title:
Songs from spirit

ISBN 1-55059-017-0
1. Spirit writings. 2. Prayer. I. Wayne,
Larry G. II. Johnston, Grace P.
BF1311.P67S65 1990   291.4'3   C90-091282-0

Detselig Enterprises
P.O. Box G 399
Calgary, Alberta T3A2G3

SAN 115-0324
Printed in Canada   ISBN 1-55059-017-0

To *Elsa Evelyn Lund,*
whose devoted
teaching truly helped us find the way.
To know her was to know of a love
so unselfish, so real, no words of ours
could possibly explain.

Acknowledgements

To Larry and Shirley Burroughs,
Tim and Jackie Tutko and
Bruce Roy Bladon,
in grateful
appreciation for their loving
support and encouragement.

Contents

Detselig Enterprises Ltd. appreciates the
financial assistance for its 1990 publishing
program from the
Alberta Foundation for the Literary Arts.

Dr. Bernadt, spirit guide and physician, as sketched by renowned psychic artist Coral Polge, England.

Larry Wayne's late grandmother, Anna Johnson, as she appeared from the spirit side to Coral Polge.

Introduction

There are many proofs that life continues after death. Clairvoyants and clairaudients, of course, need none, for they have seen or heard; most religionists need little, for the proof is in their sacred books; many spiritualists need nothing, for they have listened to evolved mentors such as White Cloud, Silver Birch, or Dr. Bernadt, have tested the counsel and found it worthy.

Others require more concrete evidence. For some, spiritual artistry has been the means of demonstrating continued existence. In 1975, Larry Wayne visited Coral Polge, the renowned British psychic artist. Though he already knew of the existence of spirit, he asked for drawings of his spiritual guides and of any others who might present themselves to Polge. To his great astonishment, amongst the drawings was a picture-perfect sketch of his grandmother who had passed into spirit thirteen years earlier. Before the sketch, Polge had neither seen nor heard of the grandmother, nor did she know Wayne or Johnston.

Larry Wayne and Grace Johnston are dedicated spiritualists—Wayne, an outstanding spiritual healer, and Johnston, a superb spiritual artist, the former in the honored tradition of Harry Edwards, and the latter in that of Coral Polge. Their first channeled book was *The Gentle Counsel of White Cloud*, a warm and inspiring model for human thought and action.

Songs from Spirit is another demonstration of life on the other side. Its messages of love and upliftment come from Dr. Bernadt, the enlightened spirit guide who spoke regularly to the Elsa Lund Home Circle before Lund's passing in 1977. Dr. Lund had been trained in Britain by Helen Duncan, the remarkable materialization medium whose death was so instrumental in the repeal of the *Witchcraft Act* and in the broader recognition of a higher and helpful intelligence. Lund, in turn, tutored Wayne and Johnston, who, with others of the Bernadt Circle, now conduct a healing mission, aided by Bernadt, a spirit doctor.

Readers should labor under no illusions concerning the subject of this book. It urges persuasively a perception of God as beneficent, of humanity as God-striving, of human potential as unlimited, and of the location of God as both outside of and *within* the true inner self. It opposes theologies which separate God from man. Man is no more separate from his Creator than his Creator's life forms are separate from each other.

Dr. Bernadt is thus part of a momentous mission. Yet there are no missionaries in the usual sense in this quest. There is no proselytizing, nor can there be, given the sanctity of personal choice and the tolerance that must always be accorded others' beliefs. There is no compulsion, no social pressure, no ostracizing of those who do not flock to the fold. If ever these elements appear, the disloca- tion of the underlying principles is underway, and an unbearable, unworkable compromise is introduced.

There is a difference between compromise and tolerance. Tolerating another's stand is one thing, compromising your own, another. Cultivate the former, suggests Dr. Bernadt, but eschew the latter which will surely weaken your resolve and dim your light.

Songs from Spirit is very much a religious experience, but it is nonjudgemental. It reveres each religion as right for the pilgrims happy within it. When it is no longer right, a new level of understanding gradually emer- ges, and so on, until the pilgrim joins the Father.

In this warm volume are some of the most masterful words ever spoken about prayer— the equation of thought with prayer, the neces- sity of quieting the mind, the key of knowing the request will be granted, the interconnection of everyone in the answering of each others' prayers. Many secrets and half secrets reside herein which were never meant to be concealed and which the slightest trial will reveal as truth.

All the Great Divine requires is a recognition of Itself, an acknowledgement of the Source of life and strength. This is not a selfish demand of the Creator. It is part of the logic of His Creation. To achieve relief from suffering or whatever problem, one must go to the Source of all resolution. It is as simple as that. If one denies the Source, he cannot be helped by It!

Here in part is the meaning of the injunction, "Know thyself," for if we do not know ourselves, our very spiritual essence, our connection with God as sons or daughters, we will always be limited, shackled by our own ignorance.

In understanding God and in effecting His promises, says Dr. Bernadt, we must traverse four levels—intellectual understanding, belief, faith, and finally, knowing within. The last is the real achievement, the God Power, for it is the perfect recognition that we create the quality of our lives by the thoughts (really prayers) we emit. If the thought is positive, loving or caring, it will yield itself. If it is negative, overstrewn with spite, resentment, or remorse, likewise it will return to the thinker and manifest itself in his life. Moreover, the moment doubt appears, an opposing thought is released, and if more potent than the original thought, it will be granted, however discomforting or distasteful. God does not distinguish amongst our musings; we are sovereign reapers of what we sow.

Hence, even the attitude of prayer, its tone, its posture, its accompanying notions, are critically significant. It is not uncommon, for example, for sufferers to grovel in prayer, to beg. But a beseeching, whining tone connotes doubt. It is as if God is the last place we should look when we are at the end of our tether, when nothing else has worked and when deep down we strongly suspect that *nothing will work.* Imbedded thus in a beseeching petition is doubt that it will be granted, doubt that it will be given speedily enough, on our own terms. The right way is to petition as calmly and placidly as possible, and then to await an answer.

Do not limit what may be accomplished, or how or when, is the lesson. Never give up hope. When you pray beseechingly you are on the brink of despair, of hopelessness. You cannot cross the bar into that faithless realm when you ask for help, for when you do, you flout one of the great laws of the universe. Remem-

ber, to receive you must first acknowledge a
Power with ability to give.

When you ask beseechingly it is also possible that you have renounced *yourself.* That
sad state too is an infringement of the law, a
nullification of your own energy to extricate
yourself from your predicament. When you
renounce yourself, you do many things—you
deny yourself, you reject the God Power
within you, and you dilute whatever remain-
ing faith you have in the God Power Itself.

Like *The Gentle Counsel of White Cloud*,
Songs from Spirit urges the creation of Heaven
on earth, and each does so because of an in-
timate knowledge of the reality of life after
death. Both White Cloud and Dr. Bernadt
stress the avoidance of self-criticism and in-
tolerance and the cultivation of patience.
Amongst these qualities, there is a close
relationship.

Tolerance of self will give you patience.
When you tolerate others for their beliefs, you
love them and are patient with what appear to
be their idiosyncracies or obsessions which
neither bother you nor spur your derision.
Similarly, when you are tolerant of yourself, of
your current spiritual status, you hold out
hope that you will inevitably improve and, as
importantly, satisfaction with where you
presently are.

When you create Heaven on earth, you automatically have patience, for what is there to be impatient about? You have it all: fulfilment is here now; impatience cannot exist.

And there is a difference between impatience and longing. You, of course, are most entitled to want things, to desire your own unfoldment, but to want these things impatiently introduces a negativeness into the works, for impatience is dissatisfaction. Be satisfied always, work, and what you want will come.

You cannot go through life living in the future or the past. To live in the past is to live regretfully and impatiently; to live in the future is to live unrealistically and impatiently. In both cases you are impatient with and intolerant to your own self *in the present*.

Dr. Bernadt has long ministered to disordered spirits in the present, to the sick and sorrowing of our world. Assuming the attitude of his Creator as part of his own spiritual odyssey, he refuses to intervene when those he guides turn the other way and stumble into darkness and despair. He will be there when a beacon is needed, when a call is made, or a lesson learned, but each soul's task, he understands with sublime wisdom and patience, is to find its own way, in its own time.

And that time transcends death and all delay caused by strange notions of Heaven. The purpose of life on both sides of the Great Divide is the same. Pilgrims who anticipate a life hereafter of angels and harps, of pleasant nothingness and mindless inactivity, Bernadt advises, shall sooner or later bestir themselves to resume the long, *active* and stimulating ascension into the Light.

David C. Jones

1

The Broad Pathway of Life

On the extreme edges of the broad pathway of life are deep running waters with protruding rocks where one could run afoul and have many troubles. The straight and narrow pathway, as commonly termed, can also be broad and wide, provided you walk in the centre and do not oscillate from one side to the other.

Thinking back, we recognize that many have tried to relate this humanistic oscillation to various cycles of time. They have also attempted to forecast the next occurring cycle, but the cycle, if you wish to call it one, is not quite like that, because each individual is responsible for his own sequence of events.

Let me give you a little example. Visualize in your mind a straight, wide road with very dense and prickly bushes on each side that cast shadows on the edge of the roadway.

Imagine, if you will, a person walking down this road and wandering off to one side, stumbling into the shadows. This unfortunate individual is scratched and torn by the prickly bushes. Immediately he reacts and scrambles over to the other side of the road where once again, he wades into darkness and the prickly thorns of life. However, in travelling from one side of the road to the other, this person crosses the centre where there is peace, enjoyment, wonderful light and comfort. As he teeter-totters from one side of the roadway to the other, we begin to understand where this cycle theory originates.

There have been times in your own life when you have felt wonderfully happy, content, and at peace with the world. Then suddenly darkness descends, and hurt comes, deep or shallow, and you say, "I must be wrong, I will turn the other way." Immediately, you turn, and because you are heading back to the centre, things improve, and you say, "Oh, at last, this is it, this is the right life." But as you veer further, darkness, hurt, and unhappiness are yours again, and you think, "Oh, I must have been wrong, I misunderstood, I seem caught. Why does this continue to happen to me?"

It happens because you have crossed the centre of the roadway of life. Everyone crosses back and forth at his own particular momentum, governed by his own understanding of the laws and his own specific ability to open himself to his *True Self within*.

Therefore, in one sense, it is true that in everyone's life there are cycles, but in another, it is not, because everyone selects the side of the road on which he travels. Some travel on the edge all the time, always being hurt, never content. Some tread between the centre and the edge where things are neither too bad nor too good. But most cross back and forth— from pain to pleasure to pain, low to high to low—unaware that the traversing is always of their own making.

2

The Greatest Problem in Your Earthly Life Today

As your spirit friends come to you, they desire to help you with your personal problems; they want to give you advice. I come to you now with counsel for each and every one, so that your lives can be a little easier and happier.

The greatest problem in your earthly life today is fear—fear of being loved insufficiently; fear of material insecurity; fear of inability to do daily tasks; fear of ill-health, and many more. Fear originates from not knowing. The only time you fear something is when you do not know. A loud noise can create fear because your imagination immediately jumps to conclusions about the cause. However, upon investigation you find it, and the fear vanishes. Fear of the dark is another. It is only imagination, and caused, as I have said, through not knowing.

Unhappily, you fear too much—you fear where you come from, what you are doing now, and where you are going.

Let me try to show you, in what may appear to be a roundabout way, the origins of these fears. Consider first the nature of your lower brethren, the animals, for there is a similarity between their path and yours.

Ancient philosophers made the mistake of assuming animals had no souls. Now, they do not have a soul as an individual soul; in other words, when death occurs with a wild animal, that part of it that gives it life, that causes it to breathe, to be born, to live in a material world, that spark returns to the group, a group consciousness or group spirit, and immediately loses its identity. This is why animals are completely controlled by instinct. When that part of animals which continues, which is life, which has the knowledge and potential, returns to the group, it loses its identity and is no longer individual. Then when another animal of the same species is born, it has all the memories of the whole group and not an individual memory.

However, when man attempts to domesticate any animal, he begins to individualize that animal. He sets up within the animal a desire to be something better. Deep down in the beast's unconscious mind is this desire to be like man, a desire to please, and, as the domestication proceeds, man brings self-realization to the pet, whether it be a dog, cat or bird. Man brings individualism to it. Thus, pets will sometimes return to you after they have passed on, because through training they have retained that individualism, and they do not wish to return to the group. So they return to the individual's spirit friends in the spirit world.

Here is a responsibility that man has—if he wishes to take unto himself any animal and domesticate it, he must also accept the responsibility for the individualization of the animal's spirit. The most domesticated animals on the earth today are dogs and cats, and they are in the same position now as humans were in the Garden of Eden.

The Garden actually existed for *many* people, and what happened with them would happen with animals if they were left long enough. People became self-aware, aware of their bodies, of their individualities, and this was the evil that was spoken of; this was the knowledge that was given, and strangely enough, woman being the most intuitive, being the bearer of children, was the first to realize this individuality and the first to teach it to man. So, now you can follow the legend and the truth of it.

However, having gained individuality and self-awareness, humanity ever since has been striving to return to the group. This is what each and every one of you now is doing—you are struggling to return to the group. Hence the great interest in after-life, philosophy, God. People are searching for a way to return to that group, that group spirit, where they can be guided by God alone; where the responsiblity for their life can be transferred to God.

However, in losing the groupness, mankind has gained insecurity. Man and woman do not feel within themselves that they can possibly have the strength and knowledge to live the life they should live—and here is your first fear, your primal fear, one which I hope can be allayed a little now.

Although the Spark of Divinity within you is originally from the group, over many years it has become individualized and carries your individual memories. However, it is still of the true essence. It is still of the Divine Power, and it is still just as all-powerful as when it was entirely the group before the Garden of Eden. Therefore, know that you are still Divine within and that each and every one has a spark of God that is as strong as God and can do all manner of things.

The only problem you have now is to contact that inner self, to contact that true self so that you can use it. But how? The first way is to rid yourself of your fears, and to do that, simply realize how your fears originated. I have told you your main fear and how it originated. Now you must think of your other misgivings. Remember that fears lead to other fears, and that they lead to action which spurs further action.

Let me give a simple example. In your daily lives you fear for security; you fear for the material things of life, food to eat, clothes to wear, a house to live in, and these fears force you into employment, work, doing things you have no enjoyment in, things you have no wish to do. One of the greatest teachers, Jesus, said, "If thy eye offend thee, pluck it out." Now there are many valid interpretations of this saying. If you are doing something in your daily lives that gives nothing but monetary return, get away from it, pluck it out, because it is the very thing that causes your problems and your unhappiness.

Now I am not advising you to leave what you are doing now and to give no thought to the responsibilities you have incurred, because that would turn your mind against your inner self and thwart you. Fulfill your responsibilities, and then begin to work out the solution to your difficulty.

You will see two people doing exactly the same kind of work. One is healthy, happy and quite content with his lot in life; the other, who is just as intelligent, is nervous, always ailing and always in trouble. Why the difference? Why? They have both the same type of work and they are both of equal ability. The difference is simple. The one who is healthy and happy has enthusiasm for what he is doing. He loves doing it. His whole self is in it. It is his very life. He has given of himself. He has this great dedication, this great enjoyment, this great enthusiasm.

Success in your material world today has nothing to do with evil spirits, good spirits, lucky charms or anything else. Success in your earthly world today is purely dependent on you! It is dependent on how much enthusiasm you can put into what you are doing. With reference to our story, the person who is always weak, sick and in trouble has no enthusiasm for the type of work he does. He wants to do something else, to get away, but he can't. He feels he can't escape, because if he leaves, he will lose his clothing, his food, his home, and so he is in a vicious circle and can never obtain happiness.

The key word in all your problems is *enthusiasm*. Become enthused no matter what you are doing, *but do what you can become enthused in!!* This is the secret. If you are doing the type of work now that you cannot become enthused in, that you cannot give yourself to wholly and completely, then first look for something else you can do at the same time that you *can* become completely enthused in, that you *can* completely give yourself to. And the enjoyment you will receive from that will outweigh the disappointment you have in your other endeavors. Very quickly you will find you are doing what you want to do, you are happy, and the world is wonderful once again.

This attitude of mind applies to both sexes. I know you ladies say, "I'm a housewife, I clean house every day, I wash dishes every day, I look after children every day—how can I become enthused?" My answer is, look at your neighbors. There are people enthused at being a housewife, enthused to be a mother. They enjoy it, they give wholly of themselves, and they are obviously very happy.

To those ladies who cannot become enthused at being a housewife, again I say, look for something else you can do at the same time. Something you can give yourself to so that your whole body, your whole soul, your whole spirit is in it, and you will feel a great expansion take place within you. You will feel a great light which will brighten the whole of your world. For remember, evil, sadness and darkness are only in the eyes of the beholder.

So, friends, I leave you now with this thought—enthusiasm—and tonight when you pray to your God, pray with *enthusiasm*.

3

The Infallible Law

It is quite right that ideas are given to people so that they may strive for them and have ambition or something to live for. They will receive these ideas, and the ideas will manifest and become solid matter; they will exist in fact!

In order to acquire these things, whether an ideal or something material, one must work for them, not in the sense of hard physical or mental labor, but in the sense that in the process of receiving what one wants one must also assist someone else or many others to get what they want. This is the Law of God.

As you go through life, you cannot just have what you want immediately. You have to work for it.

Ideals are given to your mind in order that you will go forward and not just sit and do nothing with your life. However, in the process you have to help others along the way, and when you have done so you will receive what you desire. Then something else will be given to you to strive for once again.

There is nothing stagnant in the laws of God. Everything is moving, and the moment anyone stops progressing, either mentally or physically, he becomes lifeless.

Happiness is Giving and Receiving

Is it not true that when you are happy, really happy and content, you have a great desire to share the happiness with someone else? You want to give, and is this not a good step towards wanting to love, to love each other, to love your fellow human beings? I am not talking about an emotional or physical love; I am speaking of a true love that comes from within, a true love of the spirit and of your real self. If you are given a chance to demonstrate this love, should you not be thankful?

I would remind you that it is just as blessed to receive as it is to give. If you were an individual who wanted always to give and never to receive in any way, then you would be spoiling someone else's happiness. Have you ever thought about that? In other words, you want to have all the happiness of giving, but you would never want to give anyone else that happiness because you refuse to receive.

Therefore, when you receive from someone else, you are giving that someone else happiness. He gives to you because he wants to express his thanks and his joy of living. Allow others to give, for in the receiving you will receive happiness and by receiving the happiness, you also give it.

As Jesus of Nazareth said, "Always walk in the middle path, never walk in either the left extreme or the right extreme, always walk the centre path." People who always want to receive and never to give are also stopping others from experiencing happiness. Those who wish only to take, do not have the understanding of God within them. Neither do those who want only to give.

Share Your Happiness

When you have happiness and joy, it gives us great happiness and joy also. Remember, my dears, that we in spirit have our emotions in exactly the same way you have yours; we are no different from you in that manner.

Express your joy and share it. Do not envy anyone his happiness. Always share it with him, and in this way you will draw more happiness and joy to yourself.

Each of you has much happiness to express and share, if you will only accept that happiness which is around you at all times. This is not a difficult thing to do. How many blessings do you pass by or let fall by the wayside instead of gathering them to yourself? Do not leave them, gather them up, day by day, so that you may have more happiness and more understanding of the joys around you.

Even though you may look up to your earthly sky and see dark clouds with the threat of rain, you can still have much warmth in your heart and much happiness to share with others.

This is the secret. Do not cast your happiness away. Do not throw it aside. Gather it to you, brothers and sisters, so you can have your *Heaven on earth*.

Remember, each one of you is a precious jewel to be cherished and loved at all times.

4

Have Faith in Yourself

There is a time of preparation in all aspects of life, whether in the material world or the spirit world, when you strive to accomplish something new, such as riding a bicycle, driving a car, learning to paint or mastering a musical instrument.

With all these endeavors, it appears for a time that you are not getting anywhere. It is hard. There are moments when you feel you will never do this thing; then suddenly you sense you know the answer. Suddenly it happens, and whatever you are doing ceases to be a problem.

There has been a time of preparation as you struggled along, sometimes happily, sometimes not, and sometimes without hope. Your mind and body have been acquiring the habit, as it were, and once this occurs the whole task becomes easy. You have learned the trick.

This process continues in the spirit world. There are certain things there that you have to learn, where you must acquire the habit before you can accomplish them. Always you work quickest when you have faith in yourself that you can reach the goal, whatever it is. You know you can do it, because everyone has the built-in ability to accomplish anything he wants to do.

Take the example of riding a bicycle. If a child has sufficient faith in himself, he could, without practice, get on and ride perfectly balanced immediately because the very thing that invented such a vehicle is already within him. If it can invent a bicycle, obviously it can control it.

In other words, *faith*. Faith in the true self! This is the trick to mastering all things—faith in yourself, not in anyone else or anything else.

If you have faith in your physical body, it will let you down many times. If you have complete faith in your intellect, it will also let you down many, many times. The more it lets you down the less faith you will have, until you come to the point where you don't have any faith either in your own mentality or anyone else's, your own physical body or anyone else's.

However, those who have faith in the true inner self, those who have faith within themselves, in themselves, are never let down.

So it goes on, right from being a very young spirit, or newly born spirit, until you return to exactly the same purity as you were when you started, and the trick of getting there quickly is having complete faith, without any doubts whatsoever in yourself.

5

Do Not Criticize Yourself

There are certain normal reactions for your physical body. For example, within this body there is a temptation to look at others and criticize. Then you think to yourself, "No, I should not criticize," but you are really saying, "I should not criticize because it is bad, and if so, I am bad."

In other words, if you deliver the criticism, you are implanting the suggestion into your mind that you are not good enough. Please, please, do not do this! For it will hinder you. It will hurt *you* more than anyone else.

When you find yourself criticizing someone, rather than say, "I should not do that because it is bad," say, "He or she deserves it, for I am only human." It is far better to do this than to call yourself down. Don't attack yourself!

If you criticize others, remember, perhaps they deserve it. Sometimes in life people must receive such thoughts, for it is only by receiving them that they can eventually put their own thoughts and actions right.

But never be hard on yourself. Try not to criticize yourself. Try not to judge yourself. Do not condemn yourself, for when you do, you lower yourself in your own estimation.

What I am saying is that you as individuals are your own judges. You are the ones that decide what sentence you will serve for what you think you have done wrong.

Know this—God is not a vengeful God. God is a God of love, of understanding. His love and His understanding have been so great that He will even allow you to judge yourself. He will not judge you. He allows you to judge yourself. What greater love, what greater understanding can there be? Therefore, the finest path is to judge no one. The finest way is to criticize no one.

However, being what you are, you do criticize, you do judge. So when you criticize or judge, forgive yourself immediately. For when you say, "I have done a bad thing," you will immediately set up within the "Dynamic Creative Force" a desire that you must suffer. You decide the sentence you will pay for what you have done that you think is wrong, no one else.

Therefore, when you slip, when you err, do not condemn yourself! Do not criticize yourself! Accept it and say, "I am learning, I made a mistake, I am sorry," and then go your way. If you do this, you will not have to suffer. Remember, you are not bad, you are one of God's children. Each of you is an angel in the true sense, so how can you be bad? It is not possible!

All your spirit friends are here, and we are all so pleased we can come and speak to you. The day will come when we will speak to each of you, when all is ready. There are wonderful things ahead for all of you!

6

Teachings from the Spirit Side

Sometimes we look on others and we think to ourselves, "They are on the right path, they know the truth about life, why, oh why, are they as they are?" We think and we wonder, and there seems to be some confusion.

Let me try and explain, so you will understand others a little better. As I am speaking, remember not only am I speaking of spirits who are housed in your physical bodies on earth, but also of spirits who have passed into the spirit world. This applies to everyone equally. All people have the ability to do two things: to contact their true inner selves, their own true spiritual selves; and to allow the inspiration, intuition and knowledge to come from their spirit friends who have much understanding.

If you take a musical instrument, any type, but with only eight notes, you will be very limited as to the pieces of music you could play. However, if you could extend the same instrument to sixty-four notes or one hundred-fifty notes, then the pieces you could play would be far more numerous. The more notes, the greater the ability to play. Now if a person's conscious mind, his physical mind, has only a small cache of knowledge (and when I say knowledge I am not speaking of book learning, I am speaking of knowledge of life, what you term common sense), if this knowledge is small, then his own spirit can only impress him with so much, and his spiritual friends can only inspire him or give him intuition within that small range of conscious knowledge.

If a person has knowledge of life, common sense, and a desire to learn, then his own spirit within and his spiritual guides can impress him all that much more. You cannot insert or pass on knowledge that the conscious mind is incapable of accepting. I am speaking of intuition, inspiration, and light trance states (deep trance states are a little different) whereby the spirit can only direct knowledge within the ability of the person or person's mind. So if you remember this, it will help you to understand others, and perhaps it will help you to understand yourself a little better.

There is one other thing you must understand, and that is why there are certain people who appear to be evil, to have no kind thoughts of anyone, and to be generally poor specimens of civilized humanity, and yet, they seem to receive all the benefits of the physical, material world.

God's Laws do not say—that person is good, he or she must be rewarded, or that person is bad, let us take it away from him or her. God's Laws do not work like this; God's Laws will work for anyone. The law of attraction for finances, food, clothing, or whatever, will work for the evil person just as well as for the good person. However, the so-called evil person applies the law and says, "I want this and I am going to get it at any cost." He goes and gets it; the law works for him! Now the so-called good person says, "I want that," but his make-up is such that he doesn't go out and get it because he is worrying all the time if he is going to hurt someone, and as long as he worries, he cannot motivate himself to receive what he wants. His whole attitude is wrong because he should say, "I want that particular thing, I am going to get it, it is my right to have it, and I know in my heart that I won't do anything wrong, for I am protected against it."

Likewise, the so-called bad person, if he had the same thought, he would no longer be bad either, but his thoughts are, "I've got it, I took it, I worked for it, and if I don't watch, someone is going to take it away from me." So this thinking makes him what he is.

Now when one desires something, his mind becomes very active, looking for all kinds of signs and symbols. He madly rushes forward, and he bumps his head because it is not the right route. However, this is not the fault of fate, nor of the spirit, nor God, but rather of the one who bumps his head.

When we say there is an opportunity coming, it applies to all of you and not necessarily to one single person. The correct procedure is to relax and think no more about it. In other words, if you have faith, you will not go rushing around trying to make opportunities, but your mind will be relaxed and you will know this is the right pathway. You will feel intuitively that this is the right one, and you will go through this door and it *will* be the right one.

If people are impatient, that is their problem, and until they tire of banging their heads, they must go through the experience until they learn.

Teaching from the spirit side appears sometimes to be rather cruel, but as I have said before, which is the correct way to teach?

The classic example would be the child approaching the fire. You know perfectly well there is no possibility that the child would be burned to death. However, as the child points his finger toward the fire, is it bad to allow the child to burn his finger so that he may have the experience, will never again go near fire, will have great respect for it, and will always be on the lookout to prevent it? Or is it better to stop the child before he has his finger burned, telling him, he must not do that, otherwise he may get hurt?

If the second method is followed, then the child has no fear of fire, no respect for it, and will eventually burn himself somewhere along in his life. The correct procedure is to allow the child to touch the fire and burn his finger and so remember.

I am afraid that although this may appear on the surface to be cruel, it really is not cruel and it is exactly the attitude we take in the spirit world in teaching people the true way of life. If they wish to go the wrong way, we allow them to do so, knowing perfectly well they are going to be hurt. Although they are not hurt as much as the child burning his finger, and it does not teach them as quickly. If they get hurt often enough, they will soon learn not to go that way again.

Even though they know not to go that way again, they may try to go another way which is also wrong, and so it goes, until eventually by the law of averages they will find the right way.

However, if they have complete faith in God, in themselves, and in the spirit, they do not go running around, but rather they relax, knowing perfectly well the opportunity will come and they will receive the inspiration to go forward onto the correct pathway.

As I have always said, we of the spirit cannot take you by the hand and lead you, because this way we would be living your life and you would learn nothing. You would become mentally, physically and spiritually lazy, and this we do not want.

Now I hope I have been able to bring a little more understanding into your life and the ways of the spiritual life. Remember, we of the spirit world are always ready and willing to guide you along the pathway of life in truth and understanding.

7

Life

At this time I would like to speak to you about something close to everyone, that interests everyone—and that is *life*, your life, my life, as it is now, and life in general.

Life of any description, whether on the material world or not, whether human or animal, fish or bird, is wonderful and marvelous.

Let us start with fundamentals. Have you ever thought of life as it really is? Have you ever considered one cell which when fertilized divides and becomes two? The two divide and become four. The four become eight, and so on to billions. This in itself is wonderful, yet not only do these cells divide, but they have an inherent intelligence which tells them how to form. Not only do they form, but they also become specialized. No one tells them how to do it. They don't have a small man in a green cap acting as foreman and putting them together and telling them what to do. Theirs is an inherent intelligence.

What intelligence? It formed each of you and everyone you have met and everything you have seen—the surface cells in your body, the brain, the eyes, nose, liver, stomach, skin, even your toenails, and yet no one ever told these cells what to do or how to do it.

Birds grow feathers and have special organs, and animals have different skins and special cells. How wonderful! And no human experimenter can duplicate the process. The time will come when cells will be formed artificially and there will be a low form of life, but it will be strictly cell life. It will not develop into anything else because the "intelligence" will not be there.

Even the trees and the flowers are formed in exactly the same way you were formed. Have you ever thought about this? Think deeply! Their formation is basically the same as yours; they have cell life, specialized cell life, just as you do. Doesn't this make you sense a relationship, a feeling of oneness with God? It should, because you are related.

We begin to realize that all life is a group of cells formed by an intelligence far beyond the understanding of the finite mind. This is the working of the Infinite, of God, to be united, to be as one. Look at yourself! There are billions and billions of cells in your bodies all in different categories. They are in complete harmony with each other only for your benefit, for you as one.

However, man in his material world immediately tries to be an individual, to be alone, to be independent, when his fundamental structure is collective and group-based. Can't you see that each one of you is a group? Just the few here tonight construct a whole. If there were only one of you here, there would be no harmony of mind. There would be one independent person who would also be very lonely. However, there is not one, there is a group, and as a group, there is an interchange of ideas, an interchange of feelings. Each of you has the same basic cells in your body; there is a physical relationship and most important, a spiritual relationship in the power which controls and channels the intelligence to each group of cells. This is the one basic Infinite Power, the Divine Power of God.

Therefore, each one of you is basically, fundamentally of God. The intelligence of God gives you your existence, not one of you but all of you. Now don't you feel an expansion, a closeness to the brother or sister sitting next to you. For they are *close* brothers and sisters. Can you point a finger at any one of them in criticism and not at the same time criticize yourself? Can you point a finger at any one of your fellow human beings and praise them and glorify them without praising and glorifying yourself? This is life. This is the life you all should be living. This is the life lived in the higher spheres of what you term the spirit land.

My friends, if you cannot realize this point on earth now, you will not realize it in the spirit world. Your life will not suddenly become brilliantly lit with gold. You will not suddenly know all things, for such would not be within the laws. You are here for a purpose. You are on earth in a physical body for a purpose. When you come to the spirit land, you have a different type of body, also for a purpose, and that purpose is not for *your* benefit. You are not living on earth now for your own benefit either. You are living for the benefit of God, for the benefit of the Divine Plan, the Final Cause, and, if you will live according to the Divine Plan, then all things you need for your happiness and comfort will be given to you. It is only when you stray from the Divine Plan that troubles beset you, and that you have longings which cannot be fulfilled, longings for comfort or material things such as finances, which cannot be satisfied until you walk in the Divine Plan. You may say, "How can I walk in God's way, in the way of the Divine? How? Tell me, and I will willingly walk with you."

It is simple, very simple. All God's ways are simple. He did not produce life just so that He could have fun and sport watching poor earthlings knock their brains against immovable obstacles.

Life is simple. If you are not happy doing what you are doing now, you are not walking in the way of God. You are not walking in the way of the Divine. It is as simple as that! When you do something that makes you happy and content, really deeply happy and content in your heart, then you are walking in the way of life, the true life.

You may say, "Yes, but sometimes I would feel happy doing things that I know are wrong and against the society I live in. Is this the way of God?" No. When you say to yourself, "I would be happy doing something against my society," would you really be happy, or are you being spiteful, revengeful? If it is a true happiness from the heart, you will never want to hurt your fellow human being in any way, because such happiness means knowing that your fellow man and you are one person. You are built the same. You have the same Divinity within you. The same Divinity that gave the intelligence to the cells to form the very physical bodies you are living in now.

With this true knowledge in your heart, you could not possibly want to hurt your fellow human being. Maybe you will want to correct him, if you see him straying from the path, but never hurt him. Please take this thought and hold it in your mind—your sickness, all your sickness, is caused by not being of a happy and contented mind and spirit. If you are not of such spirit, then you have wandered from the ways of God. God is warning you. God is saying, "You are transgressing my laws; return my way." And remember, the way of the Divine is not a straight and narrow path, but rather a broad pathway full of beauty, sunshine and happiness.

You can have all things. Things you want tomorrow, you could have had today, if you had but walked in the way of God or Divinity and not in the way of the material mind. Your material mind is but a servant, a servant of the Divine Spirit within you. Your material conscious mind is there to serve the Divine Spirit that resides within you. That Divine Spirit sends out the thought, the impulse. The conscious mind receives the thought or the impulse, and then controls the physical body, controls all the knowledge you have received throughout your life by schooling, experience and reading. It takes this knowledge and utilizes it to obey the command of the Divine

Spirit within. This is living in the way of God. This is living in the true life, the spiritual life.

How many of you have taken heed of the Divine Voice within you and have done something about it? How many of you have had a hunch, an intuition, and acted on it? What normally happens? Your conscious mind grasps this thought and tears it to shreds logically! You may have said, "No, that is wrong because it is not the way of Mrs. Smith or Mr. Brown, or the way someone else did it last week, last year, or centuries ago." And you follow the material path dictated by your conscious intellect. Ever remember, God does not say, "You cannot do so," but He does say, "There is a price to pay."

Now, as I speak of God, it sounds as though I am speaking of Him as a person, one that has set up certain rules and regulations and has said that if you do not do what I tell you, you will suffer. This is not true. God cannot be described. God just is and when He "likened an image unto Himself," a human being, He was not speaking of physical characteristics, but of this Divine Intelligence which built your body and which is keeping you alive in your physical body right now. When you stop and think that you have this Divine Power that can form your own physical body as it is now, don't you feel a humble pride? Don't you feel a glorious sensation within, that you are Divine, that you are God?

We are not asking you to have faith and believe, we are proving your own Divinity through the very consciousness which you so revere and worship. This consciousness is part of Divineness, but it is a servant of it, not the master.

Therefore, I want each of you to take your life and live it fully. Do not worry about the conscious intellect, do not worry about the logic. Just concern yourself with doing God's will. Feel it within, and as you walk life's pathway with this knowledge and use it, then it will grow so that eventually you will be walking in the full light of Divineness.

All the things you desire earnestly in your heart that will bring happiness to you, genuine happiness, will be given to you. God has made it so in His world; the laws of God have made it so. There may be a person who requires a beautiful home with beautiful furnishings, draperies and all the things that go in a beautiful home of today. This to him or her is happiness, but to another, happiness is the ability to walk into a beautiful green meadow and sit with nature. This is his happiness. No two people fulfill themselves in precisely the same way.

Isn't this wonderful! You are not robots! You are individuals, but individuals in a group, to help each other. Retain your individualism, but share it with all who come into your life. Do not be selfish with it. Do not stand up and say, "I am an individual, I am independent, I will do as I think with no thought for anyone else," for this is selfish individualism. Rather say, "I am an individual and I have certain knowledge which others do not have because their experiences and environments are different, and I will share my knowledge with theirs." This way both will benefit and be happy.

If each and every one on the physical, material world today could look upon themselves as one individual cell uniting to make a marvelous whole of humanity, what would happen? You would have peace on earth and goodwill among men. So, please, be a *group of individuals!*

8

Evolution and Creativity

You have all come quite a way toward a greater understanding of life and the real you. You are all travelling in the right direction. But there is one thing I would like to warn you of, and that is, never at any time assume that you have reached the end of the path and that you know all things. If ever you make this assumption, your growth in all areas will cease, for there is no end to progress. There will never be a time when any one person will know all things, for there is a continual expansion taking place, an evolution, a new creation.

Therefore, always be alert to what is taking place in your material world and in your spiritual self, and always be alert to what your higher mind is giving you and be ready to receive. Never accept any thought as the final thought, never accept any instruction as the final instruction. Always be ready to improve on any thought, any word, any inspiration, for all things, including thought and inspiration, are evolving.

In the Infinite all that ever will be now exists, but you as an individual must evolve to Infinity. As you evolve so your thoughts evolve, your inspirations and aspirations—rising to something a little better, a little different. Always be prepared to make a change, for it is only in change that true evolution can occur, and it is only in true evolution that creativity can occur.

At one time, man had only one way of travelling from one point to another, and that was by use of his two lower limbs. He could either walk or run. Then as man evolved, his creativity evolved, and he learned he could master the lower animals, so that he could sit in relative comfort astride a four-legged animal and direct that animal from point "A" to point "B" much quicker. However, the load man could carry this way was limited to the strength of the animal's back. So as man evolved, he created a wheel, and from it a vehicle which the animal could pull.

Although it had strength to pull a vehicle with massive loads, there was comparatively little weight on the animal's back. But as man evolved and created (remember he can only create as he evolves), he created mechanical means whereby he could put on heavier loads and travel much faster; then continuing to evolve, he invented machines that could fly.

Now the first man we spoke of, who could only walk and run, could not possibly have created a flying machine because his creativity would not have been in harmony with his evolution. Evolution is the way to Infinity—the faster you travel en route, the faster your creativity will show itself in any given area. So it becomes very obvious that the first duty of every human is to evolve as quickly as possible to Infinity.

What is evolution? Evolution is becoming increasingly aware. As your awareness grows of the truth in life, the truth of being, so you become more evolved, and as you become more evolved, so your creativity will increase.

Therefore, a person who lives by the laws that existed thousands of years ago and stubbornly persists in living within those laws, cannot evolve, and not evolving, his creativity becomes nil. I am speaking of the laws of the people of millennia ago, material laws. The laws of truth will never change, and the laws of Infinity, the laws of God, will never change. But the one Law of God is—to create, or to be creative, you must evolve—and you are all sufficiently advanced now to see the logic therein.

It is obvious, as I have explained using for examples the man who walked and the man who could fly in a machine, that only through evolution could the creation of the flying machine become possible. There are those who resist change, people who want to live on the earth today as those who lived two thousand years ago when Jesus of Nazareth was on the earth. They think that if they can return to those days and laws, they will be close to God, because, after all, wasn't Jesus close to God, and didn't He live within those material laws?

Jesus was close to God, but Jesus did not live within the material laws. Jesus lived unto the law of truth. He himself evolved, but humanity remained fixed for two thousand years. Humanity has remained so fixed it will not change one word of what Jesus said! There are those on earth who will not even change one word of what Moses said! They live by it exclusively. They will not evolve their understanding; their comprehension of these words has become stationary. Therefore, their creativity in this area has halted. In other words, they are at exactly the same spiritual level as the people two or three thousand years ago.

So always be ready to evolve, be ready for change, and be alert for further inspiration, either from yourself or others.

9

God and Love

I would like to speak to you about two subjects—love and God.

Love, the word itself, not only on your material world, but also in the spiritual world, love, has been used a great deal and abused a great deal.

Love of anything is a harmonizing, a coordinating, and a being at one with the person or thing that you love. True love, or Divine Love, occurs when you try to think as another thinks, when you try to live as he or she lives, when you try to be so harmonious with that person that you become one.

The true love, the true fulfillment of love, can only come when both people have this Divine Love for each other. A mental love, a spiritual love, or even a physical love is not the true Divine Love. One can love another person in any of these three senses and not in the other two.

This is why you have so many marriage problems on your earth today. This is why the master, Jesus of Nazareth, said, "There is no giving or taking of marriage in my Father's kingdom." He did not mean that two people cannot live together, laugh together, and love together. What He meant was that in true Divine Love there is no necessity for giving and taking in marriage.

However, at the present state of progression on earth we must have laws to protect you and those around you. This is why there is a giving and a taking of marriage on your earth today. It had to be so, but it does not eliminate the possibility or potential of a Divine Love.

You can have this Divine Love in so many ways. The artists, when they are painting a beautiful scene, become entirely submerged in what they are painting, in the scene, the beauty, the color, the mysticism of it all. If you speak to them, they don't even hear you. If you stand by their side, they don't even know you exist because they have a Divine Love for what they are doing. They give completely, they are at one, they can sense the scene they are painting. Not only do they see it, they feel it; they are as one with the scene. This is sometimes termed a mystic-like experience, but it is not. It is love. This is the true Divine Love which each and every one here at this time has. Some, because they have this Divine Love and cannot express it, experience little problems, irritabilities and resentments.

Take the animal lover. It is true that there are animal lovers walking on your earth today who can communicate with animals. They don't talk as I am talking to you now, but there is an interchange, an outflow of genuine interest, a real desire to know that animal's problems, to help and to become as one in thought, mind and spirit.

The animal recognizes this, and there is a return; indeed, it is much easier for some animals to know Divine Love than for many humans. Animals also have this Divine Love within them, and some, once they join together, will remain together for their entire life span, one working for the other. If one wants to go somewhere, the other automatically goes and makes sure there is protection, and then it will reverse, while the first rests and the other looks out—together, each with the one thought, both for one. This is Divine Love, and in the same way human beings can live.

The parents' love for their children, of necessity, is a love of protection; to protect the little ones until they are strong enough to protect themselves. With a true, parental love, parents will love their children completely. They will want to direct and help, not force. They will become harmonized with their children and find out their talents, gifts and capabilities.

They will not want to satisfy their own egos and their pride in their offspring. This will be the last thought in their minds, and as the offspring grows under these ideal conditions, he will return that supreme understanding and oneness. No matter how many children there are in the family, each will have this oneness with the parents and for the brothers and sisters. There will be a God fearing, loving, divine family!

Let us pursue this ideal a little further. Having learned Divine Love from their parents, these children possess it as their strongest asset when they step out into the world. It is easy for them to find someone to whom they can give this Divine Love, and when it is given, it is always returned. It is unerring and irresistible!

So you have a happy couple who are divinely in love, at one with each other. They have learned the love of their parents. They have learned the love of their fellow human beings. After such an experience, do you think it would be difficult for these people to have a Divine Love of God?

Let us take the opposite side. Take the side of a child who has not received full parental Divine Love, but rather a selfish, egotistical love. The child cannot return it. He cannot return any love at all because every time he tries, he is told, "You go that way and do as you are told," or alternatively he is ignored completely.

These children have never learned to love the first people of their environment, their parents. They go off into the world, they do not know what it is about, they get married to the first one who attracts them physically. Sometimes they are lucky and find they are mentally attracted as well. But other times they are unlucky and are disappointed.

Now, I ask you, friends, persons under these circumstances who have not found love, who cannot give love to material people that they can see, that they can feel, that they can talk to, do you think that they could give love to a "nonentity" like God—a nonentity to them?

If you cannot love the things you can see, the things you can talk to, the things you can get hold of and understand, you cannot possibly love something you cannot see.

What effect has this on your lives? Let us put it this way. In our explanation of love, we said it was a complete oneness with the person or things we loved. A complete harmony, a complete togetherness, a wholehearted self-sacrifice, if you will, although love is not sacrifice!

We are in spirit, you are on earth, and both of us exist in God. Both of us exist in the Divine Plan. Isn't it logical to assume from this that if we are here God loves us, God is at one with us, God is with us now, each and every one of us?

If we haven't got God with us, who have we got—the devil? If the devil can possess us as children of God's, if we believe this, then we are saying the devil is just as powerful as God, and once we make that statement, we take Divinity away from God. God is not then omniscient or omnipotent; there is something just as strong—the devil!

No, my friends, we cannot accept this proposition! Logical, sane, thinking people, who accept the Divinity of God on one hand, turn around and say there is an evil power just as strong on the other hand! No, my friends, this is not common sense. All things are within God, and God is within all things!

Therefore, God is within us and God loves us with a Divine Love, a oneness. Not a love of revenge, not a love that punishes us when we do wrong, but a love that is so great it allows us to find our own way, if we want to, knowing that we will learn our lessons and go the right way eventually. This is a wonderful love.

Now that we know that God loves us, why can't we accept that love, and why can't we return that love? Simple, so simple!

During your childhood and all your life, you have gained ideas and concepts which govern your actions. Unfortunately, most people consider that God is so Divine, so pure, so far away from us, that we cannot possibly come close. Our first thought is that we, poor sinners, cannot possibly approach God. But this is wrong friends. God is with you now, God is within you now. How close do you want God to be? Accept that you are a child of God's. Accept this Divine Love.

Accept that you are good enough to love God. If God is good enough to love you, surely you can be good enough to love God. To love God, do not call God love. God is not love, love is part of God. We cannot say that God is anything, for the moment we say that God is any one thing, we limit God, and we limit our understanding.

Do not limit God. God is limitless! God just *is!* And as you go your way, go with your head held high. Put each foot down firmly on the roadway of life. Know that God loves you and you love God with a Divine Love and that the

Divine Love is going to overflow to your partners, your families, your children and your spirit friends.

10

The True Love

As you put the power of God within you into effect, so you will learn to truly love, to truly love all things. Have you ever thought of what the love of God is? The true love? In His wisdom He allows you to go your own separate little ways. He allows you to get yourself into little problems and big problems, and He allows you to fight your way out and so learn lessons.

What is the greatest love a mother can have for a child? What is the greatest love one person can have for another? What is true love? True love, as God's love is for you, is to have a full understanding. When you thoroughly understand your children, as a mother does, then you have true love, for then you know when to discipline and when to encourage. And so it is with all things.

For one person to have a true love of another is to have full and complete understanding of the other. What better way to have full and complete understanding of another than by realizing that he or she is a manifestation of God, a son or daughter of God. What better way than by having a full and complete understanding of yourself, for you are the same.

True Emotion

We on the spirit side of life want to thank you for your many kind thoughts towards us. We appreciate your thoughts as we are still human, and we still have the feeling that whatever little effort we may put forward to help is appreciated by those we try to help. I did want to say this because we are not all just cold, logical, unemotional pieces floating around in the spirit world. We still have our personalities, our little likes and dislikes, for we have not reached perfection.

Do not be afraid to show your emotions, and do not suppress them, for the true emotion, truly and honestly given, can never offend anyone. But an emotion that is forced or one that is suppressed can hurt, for it is not the truth. The true emotion would never hurt anyone as it is part of the Divine, not part of the physical.

Your True Self

Let me suggest another little technique to help you acquire what you seek.

First of all, you must turn your thoughts inward toward yourself, your true self. Turn your thoughts as though you were searching for that real *True Self within*.

When you feel that contact, lift yourself out of your physical existence. In this way, you are with that true self within, and it will help you to lose all interest in your physical body for this is the ideal situation. When you have lost complete interest, when you have acquired the faculty of disinterest in your physical body, when you are no longer concerned even if you lose it, when you can acquire this thinking, it will be easier for those wonderful spirit friends around and about you to take control of it.

There is a two-fold purpose why these individuals may want to control your body. First, it will set up a harmony between you and your spirit friends which is the most important step. Secondly, those people who are still living in a physical body, who understand trance mediumship and why this contact is so important, will realize the great potential which exists to spread the word of truth and to help humanity to a higher state of existence.

When the true you is manifesting itself through you at all times, your life will be at peace, and this peace is worth every effort. So, I would ask you to find that *True Self within*, the true self that knows all things, and having found it, then your life will become beautiful.

Now I assure you that when the time comes we will help you, your spirit friends will help you, and be not afraid to call on them any time.

11

True Knowledge

There are many types of knowledge. There is knowledge of how one originated, of physical bodies, and of electronics. There is knowledge of proper behavior and of the stars and planets. But it is all one. All these forms are simply facets of a fuller, true knowledge. When one has acquired the ability to centre himself upon true knowledge, all other knowledge becomes available to him.

The knowledge of how one should run a business, for example, is just one small facet of true knowledge. The knowledge of how to perform a surgical operation is one small, tiny facet of true knowledge. The knowledge of how to operate an automobile is one tiny facet of true knowledge. If you were to count up all the tiny facets of true knowledge which you possess now, then you would have quite an accumulation of knowledge, but you would still not have the true knowledge.

However, if each and every one had spent as much time searching for the true knowledge as they have spent searching for the tiny facets, they would have the true knowledge—not just the tiny facets they have now, but all facets! In other words, there is a tendency for humans to search for knowledge from the wrong end.

We are tempted to look at the manifestation first and then to try and trace it back to its origin. In this way, we must look upon each and every manifestation and then trace it back until we find the origin of that manifestation. The amazing thing is that when we have found the origin of all these delightful and undelightful things, we find the origin is one and the same thing. Would it not be much simpler and much easier to go to the origin first and then know all the other things?

You may say, "Well maybe, but what about my personal life?" In your personal life don't you do exactly the same thing? If you have a problem, don't you look at it and then weep and wail and say, "Why have I this problem, why have I to suffer this, what have I done to deserve this?" Then you say, "Well, I must remove this problem," and so you search for ways to remove it. You look for ways to cancel it out.

But would it not be much simpler if you asked, "What is the origin of the problem, where did it begin and why did I allow it to begin?" If you do not do this, you will follow the manifestations of your problem, and quite possibly you will create another problem, and instead of having one you will have two and your difficulties may multiply.

I am sure you know that if you look in the wrong direction to solve your problem, you will only add other perplexities. It is something like the person who begins with one lie and then has to tell another lie to cover up the first, and then another to cover the two, and before very long, he does not know whether he is telling the truth or not. He is lost in his lies and so produces more problems for himself.

It is rather strange that the person who is a habitual liar is also a person who is searching for acceptance from his fellow human beings, and yet, by his lies he causes his fellows to reject him.

12

Being

No one is perfect, but then what is perfection, for I tell you now there is no such thing; it is a man-made concept. Do you think for one moment that God is concerned or worried about whether His manifestations are perfection? To worry about a thing is to fear it may happen, and when you fear a thing may happen, it *will* happen because you have the right creating laws working when you fear a thing, and you will create what you fear.

If God were to worry in fear that His manifestations were not perfect, by His very own laws His manifestations would be imperfect, and in their imperfections they would be destroyed. When you say something is perfect, you are implying that something else is imperfect. When you say something is good, you are implying that other things are evil. When you say something is creative, you are implying that something else is destructive. When you state something is loved, you imply

73

there are things which are hated. These things do not exist in the laws of God. There is no love, no hate, no good, no evil, no creation, no destruction. *There just is.* There is just b*eing*, and when you can completely understand and accept being, *just being*, not being a human, not being a good human, not being a bad human, not being a loving human, not being a hateful human, but *just being*, you will be better off, for that is all God is—*just being*. *To be* is to be with God. To be loving or hating, to be productive or non-productive, is not being with God in the true sense. All things are within God, but some are out of harmony with God. *God is just being.*

Consider for a moment Jesus of Nazareth. Think of His life in general, not Him in particular. Jesus was only interested in *being*. He was not interested in being good, He was not interested in being bad, for when you are interested in being good you are only interested in what someone else thinks. You want to be good in that person's point of view, and the same thought applies when you want to be bad.

We are concerned about what someone else thinks. Now to a point this is right. It is good for a young person to know what constitutes creativity and disruptivity, but it is also important for him to know that the real and only important thing is *to be*—*be* within God's creation. We are *being* within God's creation and by becoming interested and interested only in being, only then can we possibly help our fellow human beings. Only then can we possibly stop having false gods. Only then can we live in a true God, a true God within each and every one of us.

I would say to you, my friends, that *being* is one of the most important objectives of your whole existence. To realize *to be*—for once you have found how to become *at being* within the laws of God, once you have learned *to be* at *being*—then and only then do you find that great happiness within you, that peace, that contentment. Only then can no one else hurt you in any way, shape or form. Only then can you realize that complete love of all beings, not necessarily all human beings, but a love of *all beings*. Strive to realize this, strive to realize that hate and love are just concepts of the physical, material world. Cast them from you, knowing that you live within *the being* and God.

13

When You Reach a Plateau in Life

As you go along gaining greater understanding, you arrive at a plateau and appear to be stationary. You feel you cannot get above it, you feel you cannot get further. This happens. Do not concern yourself about it. When you arrive at a plateau, accept it. If you wish, think of it as a spiritual rest.

Do not look higher and say to yourself, "Oh, here I am, I can't get any further and I have the whole mountain to climb." Reject this attitude. When you feel yourself at a plateau, know you have accomplished something. Feel that now you have a certain understanding. Rest in a spiritual sense, and enjoy that understanding. Do not try to get above it at that moment, because it takes a little while for you to accept your understanding. Even though you comprehend at an intellectual or conscious level, it takes time for that comprehension to become part of you.

For example, when you first went to school, how long did it take you to learn the simple basics of your multiplication tables? You didn't do that in a short time. It took you quite a while, and how many times did you feel that once you had mastered a certain multiplication table you had reached a plateau? How proud you felt. How smart. But then someone came along and said, "Well, that is all right, but you still have a lot more to learn," and you thought to yourself, "Oh, dear. I thought I had got somewhere," and then you found out there was so much more to learn.

The same thing occurs in your search for understanding and truth. You reach a certain level of understanding, and then you think, "Oh, what a lot more there is yet to come." Do not do this. When you reach that level, relax and enjoy it.

Yes, by all means, go on learning, but do not look ahead. Do not say, "I know this, but there is so much more to learn." There *is* so much more to learn, but you *will* learn it. *Know this!* Know that eventually you will return to your Father and know all things.

Do not try to force yourself. Accept it. Accept yourself at your own level of understanding, and if you do, your life and your path, though they be straight and narrow, will be full of sunshine, joy and love.

14

Prayer and Praying

I am sure that you must have prayed more than once, prayed for something, someone, or yourself. And I know that sometimes the prayer is answered and sometimes not.

I am sure you have also had occasions when something just passed through your mind, and while it was passing, you thought, "That would be nice to happen," or "That would be nice to have."

Very quickly after, it has either happened or you have acquired it. You thought to yourself, "Now that is strange, I just thought about it, and in a natural way it appeared, I received it, why?"

In the first instance, when you earnestly and seriously prayed, sometimes your prayers were answered and sometimes not. In the second instance, you were not even thinking of God; you were not even thinking of anything in particular; you were not even praying, and yet, it was answered. Why? Let us investigate this so that you may understand prayer a little more.

First of all, when you pray, whether it be for yourself or someone else, there is an absolute necessity that you must before beginning prayer, quiet your mind and relax. You cannot pray to God and worry or be afraid at the same time. This is an impossibility. When you are worried and afraid of something happening or of something not happening, a dark grey aura surrounds you, one clairvoyants can actually see, and all your thoughts are inward upon yourself. Yes, even though you may be praying to your God, your thoughts deep down are neither toward God nor anyone else. They are toward yourself. They are toward yourself in self-pity, and nothing, absolutely nothing, can get beyond your own thoughts. They are just twirling around, as it were, within your own environment. You are so completely wrapped up in your own problems that you cannot possibly get out with your thoughts to anything beyond yourself.

To prove this point, I am sure that if you think back in your own life you have had the experience that when you are worried about something, people around and about you have a tendency to leave you alone. Haven't you noticed that when you seem to be in the most trouble, you appear to have the least number of friends? Sometimes there is a tendency to blame friends, but you are the one to blame because you are so interested in yourself, in your own mind, your own worries and problems, that you give off a feeling of not wanting anyone around you.

To have a friend, there has to be an exchange, an exchange of thoughts, of ideas, of conversation. But how many times have you said to yourself, "I would so dearly love to help so and so, but I just don't know how to approach her. I don't know how to get to her. I don't know what to say." Even though you know that your friend is in trouble, there is this feeling of not knowing what to do. You sense the rejection, and you say, "Well, I hope the good Lord will help her," and you pass on your way.

So, the next time you feel your friends have deserted you, just remember how many times you may have deserted them! It is not really a desertion in either case, but a sensing of this person's being wrapped up in herself, and if you are wrapped up in yourself, no one can get near.

I have said to you before that each and every one can have anything they want, anything they desire, whether it is good for them or not. This is the Law of Nature. It is the

Infinite Law. It is the Law of God. It has to be so. It could not be any other way. When you pray and worry at the same time, what you are saying to yourself in effect is, "I have problems, I have worries, or I lack something." This is the strongest thought, and sure enough, that is what the Law of Nature, the Law of God will give to you—worry, troubles, or lack of something. You cannot pay lip service to God, the laws of God or the laws of Nature and expect to be heard. You cannot!

One of the great masters on earth, Jesus of Nazareth, told you that when you pray, *know that it has already taken place*. What He was saying was that whatever you pray for, when you pray, know in your heart, not by lip service, but in your heart, that it is already so. This is the deep desire. You are not thinking of yourself. You are not thinking of your problems. You are thinking of what it is going to be like immediately after your prayer is answered, and thinking this way so the prayer *will be answered*.

Now you can see why, when something flashes through your mind and you say to yourself, "That would be nice, I would like to have that, that would be nice to happen," for a fleeting second in your mind, *you know, you accept*, with the simple acceptance of a child, that it is so. Just a fleeting second of your time and your prayers are answered, and yet, by getting down on your knees, either at an altar or beside your bed and praying for hours, you don't get a thing answered!

I am not saying that you should not pray; do not misunderstand. I am speaking of prayer, particularly prayer where you are requesting something. There are prayers of adoration, there are prayers where you sit relaxed or kneel and just give thanks for being alive, for living, for being a human being, for having an intelligence. I am not speaking of these types of prayer. These prayers are always from the heart when done correctly. I am speaking of the prayer where you are requesting something. Now I have told you how to pray—relax your mind, let your mind go quiet, forget your worries and troubles for the moment, and if you cannot do this, do not bother praying because it will not be answered.

Have you ever wondered what happens when a prayer is answered? Is there a Supreme Being, a King of Kings, a Lord of Lords who suddenly stops whatever He may be doing and says, "Oh, yes, John Smith, I heard his prayer, let it be so," and it happens?! Do you believe this? Do you accept this? No, my friends, when you pray in earnest, the thought goes out. I am sure you know or have heard that thoughts are living things. If thoughts could not travel from one mind to another, there could never be telepathy.

Thoughts are living things, and provided you are not sending out worrying thoughts, but rather helpful thoughts, you should feel confident that as you send those thoughts out something will be done. Now exactly what happens is this: Other people pick up those thoughts, not only others in the spirit world, but also others on the earth plane, they sense the thought although they do not know it, and they react to it. These thoughts together set up a natural trend of events, and that natural trend of events automatically brings back to you the thing you have prayed for.

"Cast your bread upon the waters, and it will return unto you a thousand fold," it is said. Just think for a moment, was Jesus speaking of actually casting bread on the water? Was He speaking of throwing gold and money all over so that it would return to you a thousand fold? Look around your physical world today and you will see that this could not possibly be what He was speaking of, because there are people on your earth who throw their money and their possessions around and end up with nothing.

So, this couldn't be it, could it? If this is what Jesus meant then everyone who threw his money or possessions around would receive hundreds of thousands more in return, but this does not occur because it is against the Law of Nature. No, what Jesus was talking about was thoughts, your thoughts, and He was not only concerned with thoughts of good for other people, though these are necessary. These are good thoughts because as long as you are thinking good thoughts of other people, you are putting yourself into a position whereby you can be used to fulfill someone else's prayer.

Therefore, as long as you have good thoughts of yourself, of your environment, your work, your life with others, and hold these thoughts, you will reap the benefit. A little practice, a little persistence against all odds, and in a very short while, I assure you friends, these thoughts will return to you, return to you hundreds of thousands of times, and while they are returning to you, so you will be lifted up.

Just briefly, think of all the successful and prosperous people you know. Some of their personalities and some of their characteristics maybe you would not like to have, (perhaps they don't meet your standard of honesty), but they all have one thing in common and that is a powerful thought of their own success. They don't think of failure. They don't think of need. They don't think of lack. They think only of their own success, and they have supreme confidence.

The laws of God do not have any favorites. They act on one person in exactly the same way as with any other, and even though the one concerned may not be good in your eyes or in society's eyes, as long as he or she holds that thought and has confidence in it, that is a prayer and the prayer will continue to be answered as long as he or she thinks it.

You must know or have read of a person who was at the top of the world, and then something happened. A loved one died or a close one did something very stupid, but something happened and the person who was at the top suddenly felt a lack. He suddenly felt a need. He suddenly felt he was not quite as smart as he thought he was, and what happened? Immediately, he started coming down because this is what he was asking for.

So prayer, true prayer, is supreme confidence in the laws of God that they can give you anything you desire. But remember that if by desiring something and achieving or acquiring it you hurt someone else, the law will ensure that you will be hurt also. "Cast your bread upon the waters, and it shall return to you."

So, friends, I will say to you finally, why don't you pray all day! It is simple, you don't have to walk with a mournful look on your face and your hands clasped in front of your chest to pray to God. You can pray to God right now, as you walk down your street, as you do your daily work. And the way to pray to God is to *know*, have confidence that God and His laws are around you at all times. Never for one instant think you are alone!

Have confidence and feel that your supply is there for you to grasp, feel it at all times, *know* it at all times, and you will be praying to God at all times.

15

The Secret of Prayer

Sometimes you have wants and wishes that you carry to God in prayer, and deep within your heart you earnestly and honestly desire these things. However, the secret of prayer is not in asking for whatever you desire, whether it be to alleviate troubles or help others. The secret of prayer is to earnestly desire that you will receive the knowledge, the inspiration or the intuition that will allow you, or show you how to acquire whatever you seek.

In the simple prayer of the simple-minded, petitioners pray to God and say, "Oh, God, please help so and so, or God, may I have such and such." When they pray, deep within themselves they are actually saying, "Oh, God, I will do anything you want me to do if I can have so and so, or if such and such will happen." It is not with a sense of blackmail and not with a sense of reward. Nor is it with a sense of "Well, God, I will make a bargain

89

with you—if you do this for me, I will be good for you." Rather it is in the sense that I desire it so much, I will do anything. Then the mind is open, completely open, to receive any intuition, information or knowledge that will bring about whatever your heart desires.

However, you are still not finished, because you have to obey whatever inspiration you receive, although to your mind the inspiration, the inner knowledge may not point, or appear to point, in the direction of or have any connection whatsoever with your prayer. Yet obey irrespectively. By obeying you show complete faith without any question. You must obey without question, and your whole desire in your heart must be that you will do anything for whatever it is you wish to take place. You will do anything without reservations. If you are not prepared to do this, you will not receive the answer to your prayer. So you see why some prayers are answered and some not.

Sometimes the prayer is for someone else, particularly in helping with healing or sorrow or some such thing. One is quite happy to pray that this person or another will be helped in whatever way necessary, but there is a tendency to leave it at that. What you are doing, in effect, is saying, "Please help to take the suffering away from him." Don't you think God knows that person is suffering before you bring it to His attention? If you really want to help, say, "Please God, help this person and please show me the way. I will do anything, if you will only show me the way, show me the light."

Now to illustrate, I am going to take a hypothetical case. Let us assume there is someone living in the house next to you, and you know this person is suffering, sick in mind and body. So you pray to God, "Please help this person, I am willing to do anything." Then quite suddenly from out of nowhere, you have an inspiration to go to the store. What is your immediate reaction? Is it, "Why do I have to go to the store? I don't want to go to the store. Oh, I can't be bothered to go to the store, that's silly!" So you cast the thought out of your mind.

However, suppose you accept the suggestion and you go to the store, and let's say that you see some reading matter or perhaps some fresh fruit, and you say to yourself, "That person who lives next door to me may just like that, he may enjoy it." So you purchase it, return home and give it to him. This is all he needed, someone to take note and to care a little. This may very well have been all that was wrong with him, and because someone did care a little, he was healed.

What I am attempting to point out to you is that although you must be prepared to do anything to receive what you want, the first thing you are asked to do you question. So carry your prayer to God, know what you want, whether it concerns you or someone else, and be willing to obey the instructions, no matter in which direction they may point.

Prayer is not just a matter of asking for something and sitting back and letting it take place. Sometimes this does happen, and for a reason, for you may have sat back while someone else prayed and did something about it. Therefore, you think your prayer has been answered, but the other person's prayer is really the one that's been answered. This is why I always tell you that you can have anything that your heart desires while you are on the material world or the spiritual world. It does not matter what sphere of existence, because the same law applies. You ask us to do things, and when you ask us, we go to God in prayer and we wait for the answer, and when we receive the answer, we do what is necessary.

Sometimes the answer will come quickly and sometimes not. But it is not God holding anything back. It is rather the frame of mind one is in at that particular moment. So when you pray, be ready to do what you are called upon to do. When you are willing to do this without any thought of reward, but just because of the desire, the deep, earnest desire to do something, then your prayers will be answered.

You don't have to be religious for this process to occur. The very successful businessman who may not believe in God at all desires money and all that goes with it. His mind is constantly open for inspiration. But he doesn't call it inspiration, he calls it common sense, and without hesitation, he obeys, he acquires unto himself whatever he desires.

Sometimes such people acquire things they don't consciously desire, but rather things they fear. Fear is the same thing, because if you fear something is going to happen, you are sure it is going to happen, you are so afraid it is going to happen—this is a prayer and God will answer it. God does not judge, God gives you what you call for. Most assuredly, you decide what you want, what is good for you and what is not good for you! The entire decision is yours. The responsibility for your whole life is yours, no matter what sphere of existence you are in at the time. Isn't this wonderful? Each one is responsible for whatever happens to him.

You will find, if you pray for someone else, earnestly and honestly and await the answer, you will be instrumental, whether knowingly or not, in a change of thought in that person. When this change of thought takes place, whatever you desired or prayed for takes place too.

So life is simple. Nothing is difficult in your lives, if you will only obey the natural laws. Within the laws of God, nothing is difficult, everything is so simple. Each person is obeying now the word of God, each of you is having every prayer answered. The things you desire deep down within yourself are being provided all the time. If you can do it when you are not thinking about it, think how much stronger, how much quicker it would be, if you did it when you were thinking about it.

Allow your conscious mind to be your servant, not your master. The moment you allow your conscious minds, your thinking minds, to become the master, that is the moment you are in trouble, that is when you start to digress. But when you listen to the word of God, the voice of God, the inspiration within, and obey, using your thinking minds, your mentalities, to put into effect the word of God, then your conscious minds become the true servant and you receive what you desire.

I hope I have been able to help you understand a little more and to live the simple life, for the simple life is not living isolated from everyone and meditating. It is a full life, a life of action, a life of one pleasantness after another, a life of contentment, full of purpose. This is the simple life.

16

Intellectual Understanding, Belief, Faith, and a Deep Inner Knowing

I would like to speak to you about, first, an intellectual understanding, second, belief, third, faith, and fourth, a deep inner knowing. All of you have an intellectual understanding of a philosophy, and your intellect accepts that there is something greater than yourselves: a power, a force, a God, a Divine Father. This you intellectually accept.

Why? Why accept it? Have you seen God? Have you held God by the hand? Have you seen the power of God? You may say, "Yes, I have seen the wonders of nature, the beauty of the trees, the grass and the flowers. I have seen the birds that fly and I have heard them sing. A new baby is born, an egg is hatched. Is this not the power of God?" Do you intellectually accept God because of these things?

Could not these things be natural? Could they not be just a natural evolution of the amoeba? They could be; as a matter of fact, they are. So by your statement you are not proving God, you have not seen God and you do not know God. But you intellectually accept God! You do because you feel within yourself that you are not sufficient unto yourself.

In other words, you must have something or someone whom you can turn to in time of trouble or doubt, and so intellectually you build up a theory of a Greater Being. Once this theory is established, heaven help anyone who may try to take this crutch away from you. Let anyone try and tell you there is no God or Power, and you would immediately attack—mentally, and if necessary, physically. We have seen this phenomenon through the ages. History shows us that men and women have fought, have murdered for their belief in God.

I want you to note that they have fought for their *belief* in God. They did not fight for God, they fought for their belief in God, because their belief was a crutch for them. Their belief was a leaning post. It was something they could turn to at any time. It was something that could give them strength when they needed it. It was an intellectual acceptance of a Supreme Being, not for the sake of the Being, but for the sake of their own lives and their own courage.

Yes, my friends, how many of you have the same problem? Many of you intellectually accept life after death. You intellectually accept that your personality will continue when your physical body has come to the end of its time, when it is worn out or destroyed accidentally.

Many of you go further. Many of you believe that you will live after death. Why believe? Why believe that you will live after you have died physically? Everyone deep down wants to live forever. This is part of the urge of procreation. This is where your mind accepts the fact that one day your physical body will die, but you will live on in your children. Self-preservation—is this the reason you believe you will live in another sphere of existence after your physical body has decayed and gone back to its primary substance?

I bring these questions to you for one reason. I have explained how these acceptances and beliefs exist and now each one of you must, of necessity, ask yourself, "Do I accept them for intellectual reasons? Do I believe them because I want to think I will live forever?" You must ask yourself, because if it is only an intellectual acceptance and only a belief in your mind, then you will never receive the full benefit of what any philosophy or religion has to offer you. Do you realize what I am saying? Do not walk in fear, have faith.

Faith is the *first* step toward **true knowing within.** Think of all the things you do throughout your daily lives where you have an absolute faith, and yet, many things that you have an absolute faith in often let you down. Look at a few examples. You walk into your home when it is dark, and without any thought, without any intellectual thinking, without any logical reasoning whatsoever, you touch a little toggle, and you have implicit faith that a light will appear in your home. You do this without any question whatsoever. This is faith! How many times have you done this and because of some mechanical trouble the light did not appear? But does this stop you from doing exactly the same thing the next time you walk into your home in the dark? No!

But why have a faith like this in something that may let you down? Something that you should not have faith in. I am not saying that you must worry when you walk into your home as to whether you are going to have light or not. What I want to do is show you a simple faith that each one of you here now possesses. You came to this place at this time knowing someone would be here, having faith that someone would talk to you, having faith that messages of help would be given to you. Did you stop and say, "Will there be anyone there? Will anyone speak to me?" No, you came! You had faith! A simple faith! You know without thinking that this is so, and yet, if someone were to say to you, "Is there a God?" how many would answer, "Well, I believe there is. I believe there is something. My experiences lead me to believe there is a Great Power that keeps the planets and stars on their courses, that causes birth in all things, that gives life to all things—I believe."

But why not have the same faith in God as you do in your mechanical light? If someone says to you when you walk home tonight, "Will the light come on?" you would not stop and say, "Well, my belief leads me to think that it might, I think it will." You don't stop and talk like this. You say, "Yes, certainly, of course," without any hesitation. But, as I have pointed out, the same thing you have implicit faith in has let you down many times, and yet there is not one person who can honestly and justly say that God, or the Fourth Power, or the Force, or the First Cause, ever let him or her down.

We don't care what you call it; it is entirely up to you, and I can assure you that God, or the First Cause, or the Power, doesn't care what you call it either. You may say to me, "Yes, there is not an instance where I could think that I can honestly prove that God has let me down, but at the same time, there is not an instance where I can prove that God did not let me down." You may say that. I have one answer for you if you say that—are you alive today? Is your body functioning? Is your mind functioning? Are you functioning? Did you do this alone? Is not this the God Power within you functioning in your cells, your muscles, your bones, your hair? Did not one of the masters tell you that every hair on your head is counted? Now, he did not mean to say that God is sitting somewhere up in a large room with lots of files and that He can go to your file, take it out and say, "Oh, yes, John Smith, you have seven million hairs!" He did not mean this; what he meant was that not a hair on your head grows without the force of God in it, and therefore God must know of it, and so it is true that every hair on your head is counted. Simple, so easy to understand— *faith!*

Now there comes a fourth step, which is knowing, *knowing within*. The knowing within is the God Power within you, the spirit. I am sure that each one of you must have experienced that one instant in your lives when your conscious intellect and your spirit within were flush. For example, when something was going to occur, or there was something you wanted to know, and in an instant, *you knew*. You knew without any logical thinking, without any reading on the subject, without any other possible way. *You knew within*, and at that moment, you would have argued with anyone. You didn't know why it happened, you didn't know why you knew the truth, but you knew it; you had that *knowing within* which is the true sign of a person who walks with God.

Spiritualism, as you term it, is not a philosophy that teaches you that there are thousands upon thousands of people who have passed on and are ready to take your cares and your worries and your troubles and live your life for you. This is not so.

Spiritualism is a philosophy that proves to each and every one who wishes to accept, that you will continue to live, your personality will live on, after your physical body has decayed and gone. The philosophy also goes to prove that this is so, not that those who are living in the so-called spirit world might live your lives, but rather, that we of the spirit might help you in your troubles, might share your happiness and your joys, but only so that your mind may become a little clearer, so that it can cast out worries and doubts, so that eventually and more quickly you will come to this one-ness with the spirit, the God within you. This is the philosophy.

This is what we of the spirit are striving to do for you. We are striving to make life physi-cally, materially, a little easier for you. We are striving to give a little advice and to teach you the true laws of God or nature so that you yourself may one day be with God. Not neces-sarily after your physical death, but we much prefer to see this take place *before* your physi-cal death, while you still exist on the material world, so that each and every one can ex-perience *Heaven on earth* as was promised to you. You can experience *Heaven on earth* right now, if you want!

So remember, "Intellectual Acceptance," "Logical Belief," "Faith," and "Knowing Within"—of these four there is only one that you require, and that is the fourth, *knowing within*, and the way to obtain it is to have the simple faith that you have in your daily lives with your everyday things.

17

Spiritual and Material Walks

As I was standing here watching the proceeding, it occurred to me how these spiritual walks animate you, how immediately your faces take on a different expression. Your eyes become more alert. There is an enthusiasm, a desire to see everything, to miss nothing. I even noticed one person bend down and caress the flowers; she thought how wonderful and beautiful they are.

I thought to myself, why not do exactly the same thing in the sphere where you exist now, your material world, because that sphere is just as important for the whole manifestation of God as the sphere where you take your spiritual walks.

For most people on the material world there is a feeling that, "Oh, this horrible earth with all its problems, all its evil, there can't be anything good; let me go and dwell in a place where they have evolved or come to an understanding of non-evil."

But when you take a walk in the countryside of your world, don't you see the flowers, the trees and the grass? Is there evil there? No, of course not. There is only God's creative force.

While you take your spiritual walks, you open yourselves to receive a vibration of love and all that surrounds you. But when you take a material walk, you close yourself and just observe with your eyes.

So from now on, when you take a material walk, open yourself in the same way you do when you take your spiritual walks. Sense the harmony, the vibrations and the life—God's life emanating from the flowers, from the trees, from the birds, from the animals, and sense the same expectancy, the same harmony with the things of your material world.

When things are troubling you in your daily life and you are having problems, remember your spiritual walks and say to yourself, "I am in a sphere of existence now where I am having a spiritual walk with God." When you go for your spiritual walks, you are looking for love, peace, harmony. Why not do exactly the same on earth, for surely your physical body does not stop you from being a spirit, or does it?

When you look for love, peace, or harmony and when you expect to receive it, when you know that it does exist, then no matter what sphere of existence you are in, you will find it. So I would have you take the experiences of your spiritual walks and apply them for practical use in your present state.

Lift your world into the spiritual world, and do not look on it as being something less, for surely nothing of God's creation can be less than any other thing in creation.

18

Rituals, Tolerance and Understanding

There is an old notion that when I am happy, the Great God must be happy. If I show him my pleasure, He is pleased with me. Although not consciously connected in any way whatsoever with religion or with God, there is still subconsciously a desire to force happiness upon oneself so that the Great God will be happy and shower down blessings.

Consequently, dances originated from early man's attempt to please his God. But as some danced, storm clouds appeared, lightning struck, certain ones were killed, fires started in the forest, and people burned to death. So there were individuals who thought dancing was not the answer.

The next stage in the history of man was the thought that maybe God wants us to expand ourselves, to multiply, and thereby make Him happy and not wrathful. So there came the ritual in all religions of survival of the species or the begetting of children. Even today in your churches there are the ceremonies of marriage, baptism and communion, all originating from the thought of pleasing God, or from the desire to eliminate oneself from the possible vengeance of the Great Supreme Being! This concept also proved to be incorrect, so there were individuals who took another view—maybe God thinks that there are evil people on the earth, and if so, I should destroy them, and then God's light will shine upon me.

I do not have to remind you that this thinking still exists. There are those who say, "My religion is the only correct religion, my religion is the right religion, all others are wrong and should be destroyed." Isn't this the same thing as saying—"Maybe there are some evil people on this earth, and if I annihilate them, God will smile on me and shower down his blessings?"

Then early man thought, "No, this is still not right; maybe if I torment myself, maybe if I mutilate myself, then the Great Supreme Being will shower down His blessings." Another practice thus came into being, and it still exists, not only in the East but here in your own country. As you progressed, you learned that hurting yourself physically doesn't do much good. But how many of you mutilate yourselves mentally by your worries and your fears? How many of you worry whether you did something wrong? You spoke a sharp word, you judged someone and you worried, "Did I do right, did I do wrong? I must have done wrong, and I know deep down inside God will punish me for it!" Isn't this the same thing as mutilating yourself physically?

I suggest you eliminate all these concepts from your subconscious minds. I can only help you here by creating a greater understanding, for once understanding occurs, the reaction to your fears will cease. Each one of you lives in fear, the fear of being human, the fear of insecurity, the fear of being outside of God.

Then there were those in the early days who developed all types of rituals, of making certain signs, of crossing a tree branch a certain way, or bowing to the rising sun, the giver of all life as they thought, and many more rituals. These rituals have come down through the ages and are in your churches and outside them.

Even in organizations where philosophy and religion do not exist there are still various rituals. Now those rituals that harm no one are good, and I am not saying for a moment that you must stop them. No, never! They are part of you, they have been part of you for thousands and thousands of years. They are built into you, they have passed down to you from your forbears. They are part of your mind, part of your body and part of your consciousness. If you were to try and stop them now, you would cause further frustration within yourself, and by and through frustration cause mutilation to yourself even more.

No, rather I would say, cast away those rituals that are harmful to others. Turn that energy, that mental energy, into a further ritual that is harmless. When you have found one that gives you content of mind, then stay with it until such time as your mind develops further, and as your mind develops, so you will need to change your ritual.

This brings me to religions of today. The first question when one speaks of religion is always, "Which religion is the truth? Which religion is for me? The answer to those two questions is exactly the same—*all religions are truth and all religions are for you!*

Now let me explain this a little further. I would like to speak to you of the group instinct, and this group instinct will not be denied! Various people of various mentalities form themselves into groups, not only religious, but also intellectual groups.

For example, you won't often find a doctor or a university graduate mixing intellectually and socially with the manual laborer, who through no fault of his own and with nothing to be ashamed of, does not have the education and has to work with his hands. Because there is no mutual awareness, there is no common bond.

Each one due to his background, his environment, his childhood and his hereditary traits has certain thoughts. His mentality can only accept certain things. For example, there are some people who are quite intellectual from a worldly point of view who cannot accept certain things; their mentality will just not accept them, and since they must belong to something, they group themselves and belong to a certain religion.

For these individuals, in all senses—material, spiritual, and Divine—that religion is truth for them. If in their particular state of growth, their particular state of understanding, there is no other religion, then that is their religion and no one but no one must interfere with it. No one must try to take them away from it. When they are ready or when they have developed their mental and spiritual awareness, then they will move themselves without any effort. As the East Indian Yogi says, "When the pupil is ready, the master will appear," and so it occurs in life, all life.

When people are ready to stray from their own religion, there is always someone or something, a book or something, placed in their way which they pick up, and they gravitate toward another religion. So it is a matter of spiritual awareness, and just as once when humanity became consciously aware of itself when it came out of the Garden of Eden, so now each and every one today is in a second Garden, for you are preparing the way for humanity to become spiritually aware.

Some of you may say, "Please hurry the day that this may take place," but let us stop and think. What has humanity done with its conscious awareness? Will it do the same thing with spiritual awareness? You say, "No, this cannot be," but it can be! There are individuals who already have spiritual awareness, and instead of using it for the betterment of mankind they have fallen into the same trap as prehistoric man fell into. They have said, "I have spiritual awareness, I must look after it, I must keep it to myself, for if I spread it around, the Great God may punish me!"

So they start the same journey—sacrifices, mutilations, rituals—and until this process ceases in the individual, and it will only cease through understanding, spiritual awareness for everyone will not take place. Even when it does occur, the majority will still have these feelings that will cause them to go through the same cycle mankind has experienced in the past thousands of years, in exactly the same way.

So, we now see that there is a necessity in human life for all religions, for as your mentality is and your spiritual awareness is, so you must belong to a particular religion that appeals to your makeup, your emotional self, and your spiritual self.

Now you understand why I say to you that all religions are truth, all religions are for you! You cannot possibly say at any time with any truth that a particular religion is wrong, but what you can say with truth is that such and such religion is not true for you, but may God bless all those it is true for. If you can do this for the rest of your life, others will take notice and they will recognize your truth just as you have. They may argue with it. They may try to reject it mentally and logically, but deep down they will know it is truth.

So this wisdom will spread, and as it spreads, throughout the whole of your world will come *tolerance*—tolerance of another's belief, tolerance of another's thought, tolerance of another's mind, tolerance of another's individuality. As this virtue spreads, so peace and understanding spread, and spiritual awareness blossoms.

As this spiritual awareness blossoms in its true self, so *Heaven on earth* begins to take place. Your wars cease, your jealousies cease, your fears cease. You no longer fear another religion because you no longer fear that it might be the right religion and that all the people who belong to it may go to Heaven and you to the other place! That fear is eliminated completely!

Now that you understand, if you would know truth, know all religions. Know them all, for each and every one of them is part of the truth. They are part of the life cycle of the human race. As your tolerance spreads to religion, so it will spread to your neighbor, to your family. Tolerance is neither the ability to be placid, nor to sit down and let everyone around you take advantage. This is not tolerance; it is fear of hurting another and as a result, of having God punish you!

Tolerance is understanding—knowing what that person does, what he believes, is truth for him now! You do not try to interfere with him. You do not try to change him, but you do stand ready with an open hand when he is ready to move forward. This is true tolerance! True tolerance is understanding!

Great philosophers of the past and the present have always preached tolerance. Now you can see why it is so important to the religious life. Tolerance with practice will bring to you understanding of the other person, and as you understand him or her, so you will begin to understand yourself.

The master whom you know as Jesus, did He not say many years ago, "If you would know God, know yourself"? Why is it that such wonderful teachings from such inspired individuals are ignored, and such petty things as the breaking of bread and the drinking of wine are praised and uplifted and made much of?

How many people have taken just five minutes of their time each day to know themselves, and yet each one is searching for God!

If you would know God, know yourself! People, humanity, are so busy searching for God that they pass Him on the wayside. So in the future instead of searching, stop and look on the wayside, for no matter where you look, there you will see God.

19

Suffer Little Children

I would like to take a saying from the Bible and explore it, because it is so simple that one is liable to pass by without realizing the inner teaching. I am sure you all recall that Jesus said, "Suffer little children to come unto me, for of such is the Kingdom of Heaven."

Now, everyone wants to enter the Kingdom of Heaven. Does this mean that we have to become as a child before we can enter Heaven? I know many of you are parents, and at the thought of becoming as one of your children you immediately reply, "God forbid," because there is their mischief, their little devilments. But at the same time these characteristics endear them to your heart. No, Jesus was not referring to their physical appearance or their physical character, but to their inner selves. How many parents have taken the trouble to watch a child to try and discover that child's inner self, which when he is young is very plain to see?

A child can sit down in the centre of a completely bare room where there is no furniture, nothing on the walls just light, nothing on the floor, no thick carpets, rugs or any other things people on the material world find so necessary, and, sitting there, that child can turn that room, bare though it is, into a fairy castle. It can become a chariot with white horses galloping with all the thrill of the wind rushing past the child's head. To a child this is real, he feels it, it is so with him. Then the room can become a jungle with all kinds of animals that one does not need to fear, for in the child's mind all these animals are friendly. Then the room can change again, and the child can have all kinds of little playmates, little red Indian boys and girls, white boys and girls, all races, and they are all playmates. There is no hate, no fear, as they play together.

You say, "Yes, but this is a dream world, not the real world." I say to you, how do you know this is not the real world? Can you remember when you had these so-called dreams? Can you remember when you could sit anywhere and have these wonderful realities occur to you, or has the memory dimmed? Have you forgotten, and if so, what makes you the authority?

Again, Jesus was not referring to this ability of imagining, nor in particular, to a child's natural clairvoyance. All children, very quickly after they are born, are clairvoyant. They are also clairaudient. They can see another dimension, they can hear and never question. They accept it and this is what Jesus was referring to—the ability of a child to accept without question. The ability of a child to say, "This is so, I see it, I hear it, why should I doubt it?"

Just imagine if as you grew up you maintained this faith, this belief in your material surroundings, in your material everyday life, this ability to accept without question. Maybe some of you think you accept without question, do you? How many are questioning in their minds whether this is the instrument speaking or the spirit speaking? Does it matter? If what the voice is saying is truth, if it is logical, if it is acceptable, does it matter where the voice belongs? Can you not accept the voice as a child would accept it? Can you not accept the teachings of Jesus? Can you not accept the fact that you are just as close to Heaven right at this moment as you ever will be?

This earth to a child is Heaven. On earth, after one has grown up, all one can see is fighting, arguing, struggling or trying to beat the next man or woman, trying to follow the law of survival of the fittest. But this is

Heaven, this is one of "my Father's mansions," as Jesus said. It is just another sphere, another existence, another part. If you could think of an orange—when you take off the outer skin there are sections, millions of them—so it is with God's house.

Do you see children fighting, struggling for survival of the fittest? You may say, "Yes, I have seen them do it, we see them today doing it." No, you do not! You have never in your life seen a child fight this world, struggle and try to follow the law of survival of the fittest. All you have seen is what has been implanted into that child's mind by the adults around him. When you judge a child after he has grown up and become conscious or intelligent, you are not judging that child, you are judging yourself and your fellow human beings, because what that child has become is what the adult world has made him.

Originally, that child accepted life as it was. He accepted his father; he did not question the fact. He accepted his mother; he did not say, "Is this my mother, I don't believe this is my mother, it doesn't make sense for this to be my mother; it's not logical, it doesn't follow my conscious laws." He did not say stupid things like that. He accepted. He had faith. He believed. A simple faith, a simple acceptance, a simple belief.

Let us take this a little further. Suppose each and every one of you said, "As of now I will become as a little child, I will accept the world as I see it, I will see beauty in this world, I will see love, I will accept my neighbors as my brothers and sisters without question." You may think, "But this is so hard to do." Is it? It is no more difficult than making any other decision.

All you have to do is make up your own mind about what you like and what you dislike and accept everything as a part of God, accept everything as being in Heaven. So simple to become as a child, it is so simple, and yet there is a fear, and the fear is that if we become as children, there will be a loss of intelligence, of logic, of the ability to question. Why do you want to question? Why do you want to approach everything logically? Why must it fit with your particular theories? Why? Because there is always the fear that someone may come along and make you look foolish.

I ask you a straight question. If you can answer it honestly to yourself, you will have made a great step forward. In your life today, which is the most important—to become a child of God's and enter into the Kingdom of Heaven, or to have another human being think that you are foolish? Which is the most important to you, each and every one of you?

You know in my work on this side of life, the spirit side, many times I am called to help people who have passed into this phase of existence, particularly those who have passed with an illness. Passing is simple. It is nothing to be sad or sorry about. There is a lapse of consciousness, and then there is a regaining of consciousness. Those of you who have had the experience of fainting in your physical bodies have had the experience of death. It is as simple as that! You lose consciousness, and after a short while you regain consciousness.

When these people regain consciousness, we try to have them as close as we can to something they are familiar with in the material world. Where I work, in most cases, it is in the form of a hospital and they are continued with treatment. We continue with medicines they can actually hold and drink and touch and smell. Eventually and slowly, we try to bring to them the realization, the fact, that they are no longer within what you term the material world, and this is the amazing thing, if you only knew the percentage who have turned around and said, "I can't be dead, this is just the same as it was on earth; I must still be on earth; no, I can't be dead." According to their beliefs, they say, "If I am dead, where are the angels, where are the wings, where are the harps?" *They question!!* They still have that logical questioning, and it takes quite some time before they will accept that they are in another sphere of existence.

Here is another question people often ask—if the material body is left upon the material earth, what is it that is in the spirit world? Again the answer is simple. Your physical body today is made from the blueprint of your subconscious mind. Even now your scientists are beginning to find out how many diseases are caused through the mind, and this is the reason why—whatever is planted in the subconscious mind is transferred through the nervous system and immediately becomes operative in your physical bodies. How quickly the change in the physical body takes place depends on the strength of the thought that enters the subconscious. If it is a strong and habit forming thought, it will act quickly, but not permanently, because the moment the mind changes or you change the thought, then the physical body will change according to instructions received from the subconscious mind, not the conscious mind.

You have philosophies on your earth today that teach you to say, "I am healthy, I am strong," many times each day, "I am healthy, I am strong." These philosophies are very successful with some people. Some accept what they are saying. It becomes habit; it becomes a thought in their subconscious minds. It is transferred to their physical bodies, and so it is! This so-called subconscious mind travels with you when you pass into the next sphere of existence. It has been in such a habit of supplying a body solid in whatever existence it finds itself that immediately you have a body exactly like the one you possess now, no changes. When you pass from one side of life to the other, there is not a miraculous cure of all your problems—your health problems and your mental problems. Life continues in a continuous form. Only when you come to the realization that you have changed in dimension will a change of mind begin. Then and only then, will the body change to fit the new dimension.

However, why wait for Heaven, so-called? Why wait to pass over? Why not accept and know now? Why not change your thoughts now? Growing old in a physical body is just a bad habit. One does not have to, though there are many reasons why one does—to get sympathy, to get one's own way, for example. Where did you first learn that you could get your own way by becoming or pretending to be ill? You learned it at a very young age, you accepted it, and very quickly you became ill.

So friends, when you hear this again, "Suffer little children to come unto me, for such is the Kingdom of Heaven," let it become a habit of thought with you—that you will no longer criticize; you will no longer logically question with your conscious mind the things of God, the things of faith, the things of your own existence! *You are here! Accept it!!* The world, all God's worlds, are beautiful places to live in. If they were not, they would not exist.

20

Power of Thought

You have heard me say many times that thoughts are living things and that the thoughts which you send out you will receive unto yourself. Now, let us take this a little further so you may come to a better understanding of negative and positive thoughts.

When you give out negative thoughts, sometimes you recognize them as such and other times not. It is very important for you to become aware of your thoughts and to know that you are transmitting them. The thoughts you send out, you will receive in return. This is the law of the universe. Now you can understand why, at certain periods in your life, you receive thoughts undesirable to you. Only now could I tell you, because if I had told you earlier you would not have accepted it.

There are many thoughts you think and speak which you do not realize at the time are negative. In the process, you leave your mind open to receive similar thoughts from others, and so a vicious cycle appears which is self-perpetuating.

In the future, should you receive negative thoughts, just place yourself on a higher level by immediately replacing the thought with something positive. If you do this, you will quickly break the vicious cycle, and you will receive many more benefits from your friends on both worlds—the material and spiritual.

Never Allow Yourself to Regress

Sometimes as you go along in life you think to yourselves how pleasant it is, and for a time, you feel if only it would stay this way forever. Yet, if it did, you would very quickly want it changed, for when life remains static you slow down, your mental reactions, your physical reactions, and you yourselves, until spiritually you begin to reverse direction. You regress.

Look around and you will see people who have become mentally old as well as physically old. You can see where they regress, and it is a shame. For what has happened is that they have reached a peak in their lives and have said, "I am content, I have no wish to go further, I have achieved my goal in life, and I feel good." They slow down mentally and physically until they begin to regress, and yet they still feel they are at their peak. They feel this way when in fact they have slipped so much they were better off many, many years previous.

Life, God, the whole of nature, are never stationary, but always progressing. What I am striving to say is, never be satisfied.

It is nice to reach a plateau and rest for a while. There is nothing wrong here; it is perfectly good. One needs rest occasionally, mental, spiritual and physical, but after resting, raise your vision to something a little better, a little higher.

No matter how old you may be physically or mentally, nor how old you may become, if you keep this ever in mind, you can rest assured you will never fall back, as so many others do. You will always have something to look forward to, to live for, and you will remain healthy spiritually, mentally and physically.

Remember, the more you understand, the fewer problems life will give you.

Never Beg for What You Want

In all areas of your life, never beg for what you want, for when you beg, there is a feeling of being unworthy. In your daily life, in striving to develop your abilities spiritually, never beg because to beg shows a lack of confidence.

You must demand in life, as you are life! Demand that which you desire in life. Demand it, and never, under any circumstances, beg for it. Demand it because in the very attitude of demanding you promote your own confidence.

Whatever you demand is yours; whatever you beg for you will never receive. Do not beg for anything. Demand, and as you demand, know that you will receive, know that it shall be, for in your demand you put into force the power that is yours, the power of God Himself.

21

The Soul

Many times we speak about the soul or the spirit. You all believe that everyone has a soul. But if someone said to you, "Well, where is your soul, where does it come from, what is it?" you would begin to think a little, to wonder, and to question, "Do we have a soul, what is its purpose, why does it exist?" Then you would say, "These things are of God and are not to be questioned. We accept them, and it is so."

But this approach is wrong because anything that you don't understand, anything that you just have to accept, leaves a doubt within the reasoning, and as long as there is a doubt, there cannot be complete faith. A new born child, as we know, has a soul. The child is living; without a soul, that child would not be here. Where does this soul come from and why?

Now, when we speak of God or anything belonging to God we have a problem putting it in words, because God in His entirety is a completely different dimension, and the only way one can really understand is to know in one's own heart. I am sure that you at some time have felt a truth, you have felt this is so, it is true, and yet if someone asks, "Why, how, and where?" you cannot answer. You cannot put it into words because your thought is of another dimension. Words are of the material dimension or the third dimension, so as I try to explain this matter to you, although you read the words, I want you at the same time to listen to your heart, and only then will you fully understand.

God is the First Cause, the nucleus of all things, and the best way we can describe Him is as a pure white light, or a brilliant ball of radiant energy. Now remember, the moment I say this I have limited God by words and this is not my intention, but try to imagine a magnificent, brilliant, white haze that everything is within and *It* is within everything. There is no individuality in this nucleus, no individuality at all. It is the one common thing, common unto itself. Now, I want you to visualize a small, minute particle of this integral haze which is breaking away—just a small, minute particle, so brilliant that to look at it with the physical eye, if it were possible, would cause instant blindness. The vibration emanating from this one tiny little piece would be far too powerful to exist as such in the material or spiritual world.

However, it has a journey to take and a job to do. This is why it breaks away. It does not break away haphazardly; the breaking away is all part of the greater organized whole. We speak of passing through various spheres of existence, and these spheres are not as you would find in a building, where you have one on top of another so many stories high. These spheres of existence co-exist within each other, and rather than spheres of existence, they are spheres of different vibrations. And because their vibrations are different, they can exist within each other, without interfering with one another. They are all within, and they are all here now. When I say, "here now," I mean the whole of the universe, the whole of God's creation; they are all within now.

However, this small piece that has broken away from the First Cause, if you will, comes to its first sphere of lower frequency, and there it takes on a protective shield. Now what I say from here on applies to humans, intelligent beings only. Animals, birds, fish and so forth take a little different route. They are still part of God, but they take a different route, and herein lies the difference between the human and the animal. The animal has a soul which

I have explained before, but here is the major difference. This particle, as it takes on its protective covering, as it comes down, begins to develop according to the protective covering, a personality!

In the higher spheres of what you term the spiritual world, we have souls walking, talking, lecturing and working who have never, *who have never*, been in a body on the material world—yet! But others, like you, have gone through this experience whether you can remember it or not. Eventually, the call comes to be active in your material world, to do some work, not necessarily to become a big name or to be a gifted musician or anything else. Just to be a human being is fulfilling one of the duties that God desires, and so, the time arrives and this little personality has looked around. It has investigated the environment, the possibilities of various environments, and it knows which one it wants, so that it can learn, help and work. The child is born, and the spirit has arrived.

Yes, no matter what your problems, no matter what your troubles today, each of you has made his own choice as to which environment he would enter. There is nothing left to chance in the laws of God, absolutely nothing. There is no such thing as chance in the laws of God, for the moment you allow chance to enter, then all the laws are broken, and if all the laws are broken, then God does not exist, the stars are no longer in the skies, and you would no longer be here.

Now, after the spirit enters the material body, there is a constant urge to return to the First Cause, a constant urge to return to that non-individuality and be part of and one with and at home with God. It is like a traveller who has left his home and travelled the world, and while he is travelling, he is interested, he is experiencing. But then comes the day when there is no new experience and his thought is for home, and this is good because it is this urge to return to God that has caused evolution of the human race. It has caused the progress of the world today. It has also caused your wars. It has caused many of your murders, because just as the urge is strong coming from within, it is being filtered and sometimes a filter may break down, and the urge may become a frustration and the frustration may translate into a desire to shortcut the return to God. And so everyone who promotes a war or a deadly fight is actually trying to commit suicide. He is expressing that inner urge to return.

In the spirit world the desire is still to return to the "oneness," to the Father, the Mother, God, and so progress continues, and eventually all these protective coverings or lower vibrations are eliminated and the soul shines as brightly as the day it left the Godhead. When it returns and loses its complete individuality, it becomes "one" again with knowledge, with understanding. And so, even the Godhead itself progresses and evolves.

Is this not right? The only difference is that in your mind the evolution takes hundreds of thousands of years. However, within God Himself there is no time. All is now. When we understand this and feel it within our beings, our very hearts, then no longer do we have to search for God, because we realize that God is here right at this moment. God is with each of you now, within that spark of Divinity that gives you life, that gives you everything you possess now. He is here now; know it, accept it.

Do you want to know what you have to do to walk in the pathway of God? Do exactly what you are doing now; this is your job. People think that because they want to walk in the pathway of God they have to become sanctimonious; they have to wear colored robes; some even think they must grow beards; others think they must go on a mountain and starve, presuming this is God's way. This is *not* God's way. What they are doing is living their *concept* of God's way, not God's way.

So, as we see a child, let us remember that in our hands, by our sides, and what we look upon is part of God Himself. Look beyond the physical, look beyond the spiritual, look right at the soul, and see the brilliance of God, and having learned to do so with a child, you will find it easy to look upon your neighbors and see the light of God, their very souls, shining through.

22

Life after Death—Part One

I would like to speak to you about what will occur when you leave your physical bodies. Life, as far as you individuals are concerned, will continue in exactly the same way as it is now. In other words, you will not become all knowing or all wise. You will continue to be individuals and to have your ideals and your beliefs.

Just because you leave the physical body, it does not mean you will leave all your emotions behind. You carry with you into the next sphere of existence your conscious memories, and these memories cause you to retain your emotions.

So your emotions, your beliefs and your ideas follow you into the next life. It is only because of these ideas and beliefs that each of you as individuals make your own progress. Without individual ideas, without individual emotions, you would all be the same. You would be a mass of robots. You would all become mechanical operators with the will of God, and if that happened, the will of God could not exist. It could not manifest, there could be no life, no enjoyment, no happiness, no love, and all these things are necessary manifestations of God.

Even in the sphere where I am at the moment, we still have our individual ideas, we are still manifesting the will of God. There is not just one step from your material world and into the will of God—there are many steps. But you as individuals now are as close to Heaven as you ever will be. Each of you now is in the Heaven of your choice, and when you leave the physical body and travel to the other spheres, there will be no change. You will still be in the Heaven each of you has manifested for yourself.

Therefore, I call on you now to strive to perfect the life you have now. Do not try to perfect the life you may have after your so-called physical death. This is wrong. It is so utterly wrong, because unless you can perfect this life, I assure you in all honesty, you will not perfect the life after death.

There is a tendency for some on the material world to think that if they develop their spiritual selves, then it does not matter what they do at the material level, because if they develop spiritually they will go to Heaven and become one with the First Cause.

My friends, I assure you, first of all, that you already are one with the First Cause, and you will never be closer to It than you are right now. Your awareness of the First Cause may become greater, but your closeness never will.

Therefore, live your lives now. Live your lives as though you were in Heaven, or your concept of Heaven, now. Do not say, "This is the way of things, I have to follow the herd." Do not be like sheep, but be individuals; realize and know that you are in Heaven now. If you cannot realize it when you leave this physical body, then you still will not realize it on the spiritual side of life.

I know that each of you has your little problems, your little troubles, your everyday affairs, and you may think to yourself, "How can I believe that I am living in Heaven when I have all these troubles?" My answer to you is, "Who said there weren't any troubles or problems in Heaven?" This phase of existence where you as individuals now reside and where I resided in the past, is just as much a part of God's manifestation as any other part.

So you cannot say, "Now I exist on this earth, but sometime in the future I will exist in a much better place called Heaven." When you say that, then where you exist now is not of God, it is not the will of God, and that is not true! If it were not of God or of the will of God, it would not be.

So I call upon you to enjoy your life in Heaven now, to fulfill your life now, and to concern yourself with the spiritual side of life when you get there. If you cannot control this part, and enjoy it, and know it to be of God and in Heaven, then you certainly will not find Heaven when you get to any other part. The key is what you can recognize now, for the new state of being will be the same to you as the old.

Instead of using your problems to prove that you are not in heaven, why not reconsider? Why not enjoy your life here now and know that at this very moment you are in one of "my Father's many mansions?"

This concept alone, this idea, this belief—if you can only grasp the thought, your lives will be changed. Although many people desire to be sometime, somewhere, so-called angels, each of you, without exception, is an angel now, in a Heaven of your own choice.

23

Life after Death —Part Two

I would like to speak in more detail about the other side, what you term the spirit world. Philosophers throughout the ages have tried to visualize life after death, and some have received inspiration or have seen parts of the spiritual side clairvoyantly. But their minds have been distracted by some of the brilliant hues or beautiful music they have heard.

However, the major and most important part of your life after you have left the physical body has passed unnoticed. People in the material world through their own misinterpretation assume that physical life is one of difficulty, perplexity and hard work. They dwell on adversity and the struggle to get to the top of their profession, and on the hardships necessary to obtain what they consider the comforts of the material life.

Consequently, this attitude has left a desire in the mind for something better when one passes beyond, an intense desire to have a

Heaven where all work ceases and all worries are finished and one just lounges around in a beautiful world doing exactly nothing.

But there is a danger in this thought, and the danger is this—the idea that we will go along with life as it is and put up with it until we die, and then everything will be all right. Now I want to stress the negative quality of such a thought. You can see that this thought prevents the progress of the individual who thinks it. He remains static, he remains at a level, and this is not the law of life. It is not the Divine Law of God.

The Divine Law of God is action, continuous action, a non-stop action—and you do not have to accept my word for it. Just look at non-human things such as flowers, plants, animals, birds, even the very ground itself: all are in continuous movement. It is then reasonable to presume that man and woman's life must be continuous movement. And if that is so, what place has the thought that one ought ever just sit and do nothing?

You are all personally responsible for whatever stage of life you find yourselves in. Whether you accept it or not, it is entirely your affair, but whether you do or don't doesn't change the fact that it is truth. Given this truth, does one just negatively accept life as it is, in the hopes of a lazier life later?

There is a certain philosophy on your material world today, or rather several philosophies, where the whole object is to sit quietly in the wilderness, on a high mountain, out of contact with fellow human beings, and do nothing but meditate. By and through this means, practitioners believe they will contact the true inner self, they will contact God, they will know the answer to all things!

However, let us look at this hope in a cold and logical way. The person who stills his conscious mind and allows whatever thought to enter it from anyone else, eventually contacts his inner subconsciousness. The subconsciousness of a person is a link to God, but God, or the Spirit, or the First Cause, or the Divine Force, no matter what you call Him, is in a way which cannot be explained—pure! The reason I say "cannot be explained" is because the moment you say something is black, you are also saying there is a white too, because if there wasn't a white you wouldn't know the black.

Conseqently, when you say something is black, you have limited whatever that thing may be, and likewise with God. The moment you say God is pure you have limited God, and God cannot be limited. However, for the sake of clarity in your thoughts, let us say that God is pure, like a pure white light. As that

Divine Essence comes through to man it is filtered by him. Remember that light always takes on the main characteristic of its last filter. If the last filter is blue, the light will be blue.

Now I say this because our friend who is sitting on the mountain contacts his own sub-consciousness, which is the last filter or the closest filter to the material earth, and although he may receive inspiration about the knowledge of things from God, it will always be tinted by that last filter, in this case his own subconsciousness. So he is not receiving true light. Maybe he will receive a better understanding of himself, but never a better understanding of God.

Life is action, all action. How can people act in life with the physical body God has given them if they starve it to the point where they no longer have the strength to raise their arms or rise on their feet and walk? Who is closer to God—he who acts, or he who endlessly dreams of a Heaven where he can sit and do nothing? Who is closer?

Believe me, friends, it is the person of action, and I say to each of you, never on any occasion envy those who withdraw themselves from the world to sit and meditate, because in the sight of God it is far better to be active and even to do something wrong than to do nothing at all.

Now the moment transition from the material world arrives, what takes place? The physical body, as you term it, dies, but here again is a misunderstanding. The physical body in its components may fall apart, but it continues to live. You cannot destroy any energy that has its foundation in God, and your physical body has its life force foundation there, just as your spirit or soul.

Yes, it is true that when the physical body dies it decomposes, but the energy continues. It changes form, but it is never lost. So for the sake of simplicity, when the physical body dies, the spiritual body takes shape.

What is a spiritual body? The spiritual body is not a body in the sense that you understand it. If you could take a single note, a tone, and keep raising that tone's vibration until eventually it disappeared, you would have something analogous to the spiritual body. The sound is gone from your physical hearing, but you still know that the note is there.

If you can visualize this, then you can visualize something of what the spiritual body is: it is a higher vibration of force and matter. It is closer to the original God Force. It is here with you all now, and although it resides most often in your physical body, it is not tied to it.

In other words, if necessary your spiritual body can leave your physical body without death occurring to the physical body. They are interdependent and yet independent of each other. So this spirit body, which is you with your memories, your wishful thoughts, is a spiritual being enclosed in a physical body, living and learning on the material world.

Now if your idea of Heaven has been to lay around and do nothing, then this you will do when you pass to the spirit world. Stop and think, friends. Just visualize that at this moment you are sitting in a beautiful meadow— the grass is like a thick green carpet, the sun is shining and you are laying relaxed on the grass, doing absolutely nothing. Isn't that a pleasant thought. However, now add to the visualization hundreds or thousands of people who are laying around doing exactly the same thing—nothing!

Don't you think that this would be an awful life to lead? No one is working, no one is smiling, no one is talking, everyone is just lying around doing absolutely nothing! If this is your thought, then it is where you will find yourself when you pass over to the spirit world. But you will not stay there very long. Soon the true inner self will demand action, and when that longing for action comes you will rise from your rest and start looking, and as you do, so you will be guided to whatever action you require, be it as an author, a composer, a builder, a helper, a nurse. No matter what it is, the action will be brought to you just as you want it. When you leave your physical body and come to the spirit world, if there should be something of a particular nature that you would like to do, such as gaining wisdom or great knowledge, then you will find yourself in a place where you can learn and gain the knowledge. Whatever you wish now, will take effect when you pass into the spirit world.

Today on the earth in your physical body, if you desire something, an action, a particular employment, a specialized ability, you will feel that inner urge and go for it! Is this not true? Has not each of you experienced how it appears to be drawn to you? You are directed to the thing you want and you receive it! If you can do this on earth, why the desire to go to Heaven—for as above, so below, and as below, so above! There are places in the spirit world that are worse than any dens of iniquity on your material world.

Oh yes, the actual fact of dying does not make you angels immediately, and it does not give you all knowledge immediately. There was once on the material world a practice whereby prayers were said for those who had just passed over and had to go through what they called purgatory. Allow me to say, friends, that if these prayers were earnest and given from the heart they would do a lot of good for the departed, because should a person pass to the spirit world feeling guilty, feeling he must be punished, then he will be punished. Not by anyone else, but by himself! He is the one who will punish himself in exactly the same way as he did on earth. Thus, if you carry a guilt feeling in your mind, if you feel guilty, then you will punish yourself, and your punishment always fits your crime.

My friends, you are just as much in Heaven right now as you ever will be! Many of your spirit friends have told you of the beautiful places in the spirit world, huge auditoriums and amphitheatres with beautiful music. The music is co-ordinated with colors which change as the music changes. These are very wonderful places that do exist, and they can be yours to enjoy, along with beautiful meadows and grasslands that are similar to those on your world, but in the spirit world they are at a much higher vibration which gives them a greater brilliancy, life and attraction.

However, you could have these things on your earthly world today. You have wonderful auditoriums and your scientists have been working for some time to co-ordinate sound with color and color with sound. The day is not far in your world when you will have these beautiful auditoriums with music and color harmoniously co-ordinated.

Now to summarize briefly, what I am saying to each of you is—never on your material earth, in your physical body, be inactive. For the true prayer to your God is for action. The greatest worship you can give to the Life Force is to be part of that Life Force! To be part of that God in progress, in action, in deeds! Never wish for death to come in hopes of a better world, for I tell you truth, friends, if you cannot see the beauty on your earth right now, you will never see the beauty in your Heaven!

So, friends, action. Open your eyes and your ears. Look at the beauty around you, and *let Heaven on earth be with you today.*

24

Passing from One Sphere to Another

When people pass from one sphere of existence to another, from material to spiritual, it doesn't follow that they immediately become what you term spiritualists. They don't immediately believe in life after death, even though they themselves have passed through it. This may seem strange, but it is not, because when you pass from your material life to your spiritual life, you still have the same beliefs, the same thoughts and the same personality.

In other words, if you were a devout follower of any philosophy, you would continue to be a devout follower of that philosophy in the spirit world. On our side of life there are the various denominations of churches and various preachers in each church, and we also have our spiritual meetings.

As I speak to you tonight, there are sitting amongst you and beside you unseen people who firmly believe that there is no life after death and who also firmly believe that right now I am talking to the dead, which is you, and they are the ones that are alive! This is perfectly true.

We try to explain to people, not force, but explain to them, in much the same way as you do in your churches, that there is a continued life. The only difference is that we do not have a church. Our little meetings are in the open air, in the meadows where the grass is perfectly green, and there are magnificent trees all around with children playing in the immediate surroundings.

So you see there is no difference between the material world and the spiritual world, unless each and every person is willing to accept a difference. You may say to me, "How is it possible for a person to pass from the physical state to the spiritual state and still not believe in life after death?" Well, there are several beliefs, but the most common one at the moment is that by some mysterious way the person didn't die, but came to some kind of fourth dimensional time lapse which he passed through. Why he passed through it is a secret of God's, and no one must question God's secrets!

Yes, my friends, people are still just as dogmatic, they will accept only what they want to accept. So what I am saying is when one passes to the spirit world he continues his life, and if he is not ready to accept the philosophy of life after death at that point, he won't accept it when he passes over.

25

Do You Need Confirmation Of Your Truths?

The important consideration in accepting or not accepting any particular concept is whether there is something in it for you; whether there is something to learn, to bring enlightenment. This is the important thing.

Past concepts have proven themselves wrong. New concepts, you are a little reluctant to accept. Don't worry about it. Don't let it bother you. It doesn't bother me. Just accept life. If everyone in the material world would just accept his daily life, live it to the best of his ability and not try to change the world to his beliefs, he would be much happier.

The reason anyone wishes to change another's belief is very simple—if he has a belief and can get one more person to accept it, then he does not feel different. He does not feel he is the odd one out. He feels there is at least another beside him. But this thinking is awry, because if we know a truth, and we know it in our hearts, then we shouldn't care if anyone else believes it or not.

Why waste time trying to convert those with their own problems, those uninterested in our difficulties, those focussed solely on themselves? Why should we concern ourselves in using our energy and our knowledge of truth in trying to change them; for indeed, we may not succeed, they may change us.

If we have a truth and go looking for confirmation of that truth, then it is no longer truth to us. By trying to convert others, we are only looking for confirmation of our own truth.

I would like to make this point clear—if you have a truth, you do not need confirmation from anyone. The moment you try to convert someone else who has not asked to be converted, or the moment you try to force your truth on someone else, then you know that you do not believe it to be a truth. Immediately you fill with questions—"Is it a truth or is it not? Why can't I accept it as a truth? What is stopping me? Why do I need confirmation?" To be confirmed in someone else's ideology is simply making an excuse, because if you are confirmed that way, you are promptly saying that if this ideology is wrong, it is not

your fault; it is the person's fault who confirmed you.

A person who walks in truth needs neither
confirmation nor excuses, for he who walks in
truth knows that this is the truth for him. He
needs no confirmation, neither does he need
company. But if company wishes to come
along, he welcomes it because a friend in truth
is a rare jewel. When you have such a friend,
there is no criticism either one way or the
other, no praise one way or the other, no
glorification one way or the other—for friends
in truth do not need these things because they
are in harmony and are one within one.

I ask you to contemplate, do you need to
be confirmed? Do you need confirmation? If
you do, be truthful; answer "yes" and go to the
right place to receive that confirmation, knowing that one day you will not need it.

My objective is to help you realize that
there are many who look for confirmation.
There are many who say, "Am I sure this is
right; if only someone else would say the same
thing." This is looking for confirmation. But
don't worry about it. None of you must worry,
for then you build up the destructive side.
What you must do is think about these things
and then ask if you look for confirmation or
not. If you do, there is a legitimate reason.
Strive to find it, but don't worry about it. Just

find it, and when you do, you will know that you do not need confirmation.

I am just another like you, struggling along the pathway, looking for further enlightenment and attempting to help those who come to me for help. I want you to stop worrying about the things you think in your life are wrong, and I want you to put that energy into doing what is right. Right not for me, not for God, not for any creative force, but right for you!

If you do this, I promise you that in a very short time you will be a very happy person.

26

Mediumship Explained

The most common type of mediumship is clairvoyance. There are different types of clairvoyance, but two in particular. One occurs when a person senses a spiritual being around him, and from the sense he automatically builds up a mental picture. It is rather like thinking of something and seeing it in your mind's eye.

This type of clairvoyant can make mistakes, for a person with this gift is susceptible to thoughts of others around him. Hence, certain clairvoyants will always tell you what you are really wishing for. They receive the impressions from your mind and mistakenly, not always but sometimes, think they come from spirit. They interpret what they see and utter messages that are not right and which do not prove themselves. However, this is not to say that these people do not have a gift. They have a gift; it is just that they are not trained to differentiate between material thoughts and spiritual thoughts. They are not deliberate frauds and neither are they trying to deceive anyone; it is just a lack of training.

The other main type of clairvoyance, which is much more accurate, occurs where the spirit person is in thought communication with the medium and the spirit guide is transferring the thought directly to the medium's mind, setting up very vivid, very clear, colored and detailed pictures in the mind. This is what they call the "psychic eye," and so the medium gives off very accurate descriptions and will give evidence which can be proven.

Clairaudience is much the same as clairvoyance and operates much the same way—the sensitive areas being the nerves of the ear rather than those of the eye. You can have either clairvoyance or clairaudience both by the way I have just described.

Then, of course, we have trance clairvoyance. It is not clairvoyance in the true sense, but is rather a trance where the spirit guide has full control and just uses the voice of the medium to speak in detail of what he or she can see. But this is not true clairvoyance; it is trance mediumship which is completely different.

Sometimes a medium picks up thoughts or vibrations from someone else close to you, someone who may be standing or sitting close by, in the material sense. This is why sometimes the medium will give a message for someone close to you that fits exactly what you are wishing for. The medium is not trying to be deceitful, he is not trying to be fraudulent; it is just that he does not understand and does not have the training.

Regarding trance mediumship, there is only one type, but many stages. There is light trance. Light trance occurs when the spirit has control over the subconscious mind, but the conscious mind is still faintly aware of what is going on. The medium knows exactly what has been said and what has taken place, although he has no control over it. But he has not completely left his physical body.

This is very light trance which will go deeper in degrees until eventually there comes the time when the medium has completely left control to the spirit and has travelled in the spirit world and knows nothing of what has been said or what has taken place in his own body. Yet in the process (and this is when you are first trying to develop trance) comes the difficulty. The subconscious mind cannot be left for a second without something being in control, otherwise it would immediately return to its animal or bestial background.

You must remember that your subconscious mind is purely automatic; it cannot think for itself. It will do anything that you tell it to do, but it cannot think, it cannot reason. It takes care of your sympathetic nervous system, it takes care of your breathing, it takes care of your blood stream and the muscles of the heart. This is what the subconscious mind does.

A hypnotherapist can take control of someone else's subconscious mind and through suggestion can direct the nerves of the physical body to feel no sensation of pain or discomfort. If he does something which would normally cause pain in the nerves of the physical body, it does not register, or I should say, it registers, but the subconscious mind ignores it because the subconscious is purely automatic and will do only what the consciousness tells it.

Therefore, to achieve trance development, there has to be a slow loosening of the conscious mind of the medium and a slow taking over of the conscious mind by the spirit person. This interchange is not a quick process, and here is where the doorkeeper comes in. As each spirit person leaves control of the subconscious mind, the doorkeeper immediately steps in and holds the subconscious mind in abeyance until the next spirit individual is ready to control, and then there is a gentle taking over by the spirit person.

Sometimes when either what you term the doorkeeper or the spirit person who is taking control of the medium (now how can I explain this without hurting someone's feelings) is not well trained and does not fully understand what is taking place, then you get these weird and wonderful things happening to the medium, where his face goes barbarian in appearance and he utters strange sounds, shrieks and what not. Now this is what happens—the doorkeeper steps up and releases the subconscious mind before the other spirit person has control over it, and consequently, for a few seconds the subconscious reverts to the animal or bestial level.

Once you understand what happens, it is much easier for you when you are observing a medium, and then you don't need to criticize because it is a simple occurrence and there is nothing to be afraid of, providing the spirit or so-called doorkeeper or guardian angel is present and knows what he is doing. This is why we advise no one to develop alone, because when you are in a group developing for any type of mediumship, we can as a group take care of you and guide you. I would like to say that the doorkeepers in your group are well trained and well versed in all phases of mediumship.

The process of learning to become a doorkeeper has to be studied after the person passes into the spirit world, and there are places where this skill is taught to those wishing to master this type of work. It is much like your universities, schools and colleges, but before these spirit people can take control over a developing medium, they have to be fully qualified. However, in lower spheres of existence, as in all things, their knowledge is not as great in their schools and colleges, and they do not realize exactly what is taking place, so they are allowed to become doorkeepers before they are ready. But this is in another sphere of existence. Your sphere is purely dependent upon what your aspirations are spiritually, and with high spiritual aspirations, you will contact a high spiritual level, high in the sense of knowing more, spiritually and materially, knowing more of what life is, all life. And as I have said to you all, have no fear for yourselves as you can have absolute confidence in all your guardian spirits.

I felt this would help you in your own development and in gaining a greater appreciation of other mediumistic people. From understanding grows tolerance, and once one understands all that is taking place, he or she can righteously judge it, and in righteous judgement there is no violation of God's law.

A sitter in the home circle asked, "Dr. Bernadt, in reference to the colorful lights that are seen in the sitting room, could you explain what they are and why we see them?"

Yes, there is an in-between stage, in-between material and spirit when you are sitting for development and experimentation. What actually happens is that the entire room you are sitting in, its vibrations, are in effect raised slightly from those of the material world. There is a slight increase, not a lot, but it is put out of harmony with the rest of the world, and this is why sudden noises or things like that are such a shock because you are slightly out of harmony with the material world. In the part of the spirit world where we are working with you, its vibrations are lowered a little which throws it out of harmony with the remainder of the spiritual world. All your senses are affected—your sight, your hearing, your mentality, and you begin to see the power or energy because your vibrations are uplifted slightly. If you could remain in this raised state as you went about your daily life, you would see this energy or power radiating around you all the time because it is occurring continuously, but out of range of the material, earthly world.

The brilliant lights or beams of light are also radiant energy, and because you are in this environment a little higher in vibration, you have the opportunity to sense and see these wonderful experiences.

We dare not increase the vibratory power or take you any further. I do not want to frighten you, but if we did take you further, then you would disappear from the material world. The room and everything in it would actually disintegrate into its basic molecules and atoms because the vibration would become so high that your atomic structure would not be able to withstand it, and it would just disintegrate.

However, a slight increment helps us in our work and though you can see these bolts of energy and flashes of brilliant light, we always, of course, return you to your normal vibratory level, as we would not leave you in that altered state.

Now I do thank you all for your loyalty, your love, and the way you have received the spirit people who come to speak to you. They also send their love and gratitude.

27

Christ and Christmas

I would like to speak to you of Jesus, the Jesus of Nazareth, because to thinking people, particularly of today, there is doubt in many minds! Did Jesus really exist? Did Jesus do the things that have been written He did, and was He the son of God, and was He divine?

Now, I do hope to answer some of these questions for you, but in such a short time I can only give you a general outline, and it is for each and every one who is interested to follow up and find out for yourself.

To begin with, there is a mystery around the birth of Jesus. There always has been, and there always will be. Yet there is a logical explanation, and there is nothing super-natural about it at all.

Jesus was born a person in a normal way, just like you and I were, when I was on the material world. He was born of the Virgin Mary; she was His mother.

Now, the parents and the family of Jesus had many injustices done to them, and the people He belonged to had been trodden under by land hungry moneymongers, like similar types living on your earth today!

Jesus of Nazareth, being of the nature He was as a young boy, pondered these things, and the main thought that prevailed in His mind was: "Why? Why are these things happening to my people?" Then the thought expanded to, "Why are these things happening to my world?"

There were many atrocities perpetrated in those days in the name of God, and they started Jesus to think inwardly, to ponder deeply such issues. But Jesus did not just meditate on these questions for a few minutes and leave them. Rather, He wanted the answers, and in searching for them, He travelled many lands and studied under many teachers. You will find that a certain part of Jesus' life is not recorded.

In searching He discovered that many of the answers to His questions were not found by listening to others, or by reading ancient scrolls, but by heeding a small voice within! He also found that sometimes the small voice within told Him things which seemed wrong at the time, but they proved to be right later, and so He turned more and more to listening to the small voice. Not only did He listen, He *obeyed*, and over the years a great trust, a great faith arose in Jesus. So through His internal searching, pondering, His travels and learning, and His complete trust and faith in the small voice within, Jesus became one of the finest, one of the greatest instruments that the higher teachings could pour through to the world.

Jesus, "The Christ," came from the occult schools of those days, and the occult schools then and some today consider that the highest sphere of individual existence or state of being is named "The Christ Sphere." In other words, this is the sphere that each and every one should aspire to, and I agree. Beyond this "Christ Sphere" one loses individuality and returns in complete oneness to the Godhead, just as your physical bodies return to the dust when they decay. In other words, they return to oneness with Mother Earth from where they came, and so, *as above, so below*, there is nothing mysterious in philosophy, nothing whatsoever; it is all very simple.

Therefore, "The Christ Sphere" is what "The Christ" reached, and Jesus became so at one with this sphere of existence that He was with it at all times, and in His later years as He preached to the multitudes. Very seldom was He "Jesus of Nazareth," but nearly always He was Jesus, the instrument of "The Christ." I am making a very fine distinction here which I want you all to note: Jesus allowed "The Christ Sphere" to work through Him completely, without question and without any doubt whatsoever. Therefore, with complete faith and because this higher existence could work through Him, He could perform healing miracles, as they were termed. Jesus did other things as well—He could cast out devils, but certain miracles He was said to perform, He did not, but they were symbolic of what He did do.

Jesus now came to a point in His life where He had to choose. He had previously been tempted many times, but now He had to choose. Did He want to remain as a permanent instrument of the Christ Intelligence or did He want to become a personality Himself and live His own life? For this is something everyone has to do! He made His decision, and the decision was a very wise one for Jesus of Nazareth inasmuch as He decided to be a personality unto Himself and live His life— and so, the crucifixion.

Remember, Jesus was a son of God in exactly the same way each of you sitting here now is a child of God. Each one of you is a son or a daughter of God; there is no difference. Jesus was not one of the chosen ones, He was not especially looked upon by God, for did not Jesus Himself say, "Of all the things that I have done, you shall do also and even greater things you shall do." But if Jesus was the only son of God, how is it possible that you here can do greater things?

Jesus knew that anyone living then or in the future could do exactly what He had done and become one with that higher sphere of individual existence and live a life of plenty in happiness and joy. Yes, my friends, you also could heal, you also could cast out devils, but you are lacking one thing, the one thing Jesus had: you are lacking the faith, faith in the God within you.

We of the spirit are fully aware that your Christmas is very close. We on our side of life recognize the occasion in much the same way as you do on earth. There is gaiety, joy and celebration.

Tonight, my dears, I have said to you two things I want you to remember on Christmas morning. When you awake on Christmas morning say to yourself, *"I am a son or daughter of God."* Feel it, know it, and this will be one of the greatest, the happiest Christmases you ever had. The second thing is: *as you accept God, so your life will open to the light of God.*

Now finally, may each and every one here, and many more who are not, awake on Christmas morning with the greatest Christmas gift of all—***knowing you are a child of God's.***

The Power of the Gentle Touch
with Larry Wayne, Spiritual Healer

Audio Cassette by Dr. Bernadt
Teachings from the Spirit Side

The Gentle Council of White Cloud

Larry Wayne and Grace Johnston's first wonderful book embraces the wisdom of White Cloud, teacher of spirit guides. Herein lies more honest hope, accessible hope, than in a mountain of murky manuscripts on philosophy and psychology. There is nothing to fear, nothing insurmountable, nothing unattainable, says White Cloud. And his soothing counsel is for everyone.

White Cloud's simple suggestions are like the loaves of bread and the fishes at Galilee with their strange multiplying ability. They are pearls of wisdom which when beheld, when meditated on and prayed about, build on themselves, yielding more understanding.

In these assuring and upbearing pages are many messages of light and love emanating a warmth, inspired, insistent and unmistakable.

Price $14.95
Available from:
Detselig Enterprises, Ltd.
P.O. Box G399
Calgary, Alberta, Canada, T3A 2G3

Notes

Printed in Canada